Penpoints, Gunpoints, and Dreams

Clarendon Lectures in English Literature 1996

Penpoints, Gunpoints, and Dreams

TOWARDS A CRITICAL THEORY OF THE
ARTS AND THE STATE IN AFRICA

NGŨGĨ WA THIONG'O

CLARENDON PRESS · OXFORD
1998

Oxford University Press, Great Clarendon Street, Oxford OX2 6DP

Oxford New York

Athens Auckland Bangkok Bogota Bombay
Buenos Aires Calcutta Cape Town Dar es Salaam
Delhi Florence Hong Kong Istanbul Karachi
Kuala Lumpur Madras Madrid Melbourne
Mexico City Nairobi Paris Singapore
Taipei Tokyo Toronto Warsaw

and associated companies in
Berlin Ibadan

Oxford is a trade mark of Oxford University Press

Published in the United States
by Oxford University Press Inc., New York

British Library Cataloguing in Publication Data
Data available

Library of Congress Cataloging in Publication Data
Data available
ISBN 0-19-818390-9

1 3 5 7 9 10 8 6 4 2

Typeset by Pure Tech India Ltd, Pondicherry
Printed in Great Britain
on acid-free paper by
Bookcraft Ltd,
Midsomer Norton, Somerset

In memory of Karĩmi Nduthi,
a fighter for democracy and social justice
in Kenya, who was cruelly assassinated
on 24 May 1996

Preface

I am grateful to the Oxford University English Faculty and the Oxford University Press for inviting me to give the 1996 Clarendon Lectures. I was received with much warmth by the faculty and students. The chairman of the faculty, Dr Vincent Gillespie, was very helpful and I would like to thank him for the dinners at St Anne's College and for the many comments he made on medieval literature, often pointing out interesting parallels between my current concerns and those of people like John Trevisa and others who used to fight for the independence of English from Latin and French—English language itself had gone through a post-colonial phase, he commented at one point. I also enjoyed talking to Dr Robert Young of Wadham College, who introduced me to the audience at the beginning of the lectures. The comments he made on neo-colonialism were the perfect background for my talks and I later discovered that two issues of the *Oxford Literary Review*, of which he was the editor, were devoted to colonialism and neo-colonialism. I am grateful to Jason Freeman of the Oxford University Press for his gentle prodding and for looking after me and my wife, Njeeri; and we greatly appreciate the help and thoughtfulness of Barbara Thompson, also of Oxford University Press. My publishers from Heinemann, Oxford, and James Currey Ltd, Oxford, turned up in large numbers and provided a kind of family solidarity. I was touched by the fact that some scholars had come all the way from my old university, Leeds, as well as from other parts of Great Britain to hear my humble offerings. All in all, being at Oxford for the ten days between 8 and 17 May 1996 was both like a reunion party with old friends like Professor Andrew Gurr of Reading and his wife, and also a chance to make new ones. In this respect I would like to thank Professor Suzanne Romaine, Fellow at Merton College, for sharing with me her work on Hawaiian Creole English. I was very happy to meet students from Africa and the Caribbean. Two of them, Ms Monica Kathĩna and Mr Njonjo, were Kenyans and they brought me up to date with what had been happening in my country. Mr Njonjo, doing postgraduate work in law, invited my wife and me to a dinner at Jesus College, and it was a pleasant surprise to discover that he had attended Alliance High School, my old institution in Kenya, so that through him I was able to connect with my past. Mr Njonjo had not yet been born when I attended the school in the Fifties, but it was interesting that some of the old traditions which I had encountered at the school were still there in his time. With respect to tradition, it was a little reminiscent of Oxford, though more recent. It is impossible to walk through the streets of Oxford without being conscious of history all the time. A huge portrait of Queen Elizabeth I hangs from the wall of the dining-room in Jesus College and it was as if it was rebuking me for my unfavourable reference, in my lecture 'The Allegory of the Cave', to her edict of 1601 in which she had called for the expulsion of black people from her realm.

I stayed at Somerville College, previously an all-women's college, but now mixed, where my wife joined me for the last three days of my stay. Our apartment was next to Margaret Thatcher Court. Lady Thatcher had been a graduate of Somerville, and again I felt another rebuke for claims in my other writings that the capitalist fundamentalism of which she and Reagan were the leading apostles was wreaking social havoc in the world and generating other forms of fundamentalism in opposition or in alliance. The staff at the lodge were always very helpful and I would like to thank the college for hosting me and my wife and for supplying us with all our needs.

I have gained a lot from my colleagues in the Departments of Comparative Literature and Performance Studies. When Professor Manthia Diawara and I worked on a documentary film, *Sembene: The Making of African Cinema*, we talked a great deal about black aesthetics and the concept of oral *mise-en-scène* which was important for the fourth lecture on orature and europhone glory. The second lecture, 'Enactments of Power', provoked a lively discussion during a session of the faculty colloquium of the Performance Studies Department. I would like to thank those who took part: Professors Barbara Browning, Barbara Kirshenblatt-Gimblett, May Joseph, José Muñoz, and Richard Schechner, as well as two visiting professors, Annabelle Melzer and Ann Daly, a visiting scholar, Professor Kristof Tlesnirovicz, and Professor Carol Martin of the Drama Department. The lecture has benefited from their very generous comments, suggestions, and questions. Professor Timothy Reiss took the time to read all the lectures and made very useful comments on many aspects of them, particularly on the question of the alliance of power and literature in society. Dr Maarten van Delden shared with me the current state of research on Shakespeare's Caliban. The theme of the development of modern literature in African languages underlies the entire lecture series, and by way of comparison and encouragement, Professor Daniel Javitch has often made his time available for discussions on language and the rise of national literatures in Europe. Professor Carol Sicherman of Lehmann's College has always been generous with sources and has sent me all the references she could find on the earliest uses of the term 'orature' by the late Pio Zirimu. I am grateful to New York University and to the Dean of the Faculty of Arts and Sciences for the support of *Mūtiiri*, a journal of modern literature and culture in the Gīkūyū language. To my knowledge it is the first of its kind in an African language to be supported and housed in a major department in a leading institution of higher learning. The writers and publications it has already inspired gives me the faith, courage, and conviction that there is great future in literature in African languages. I do not have to argue about this to sceptics at literary conferences; I can now demonstrate the possibilities of what I am advocating in the fourth lecture and in my other publications on the language question in Africa. And lastly, I owe a word of gratitude to the chairs of the two departments, Professor Jennifer Wicke and Professor Peggy Phelan, who were understanding about my absence at that time of the year.

I would like to thank my students at the Departments of Comparative Literature and Performance Studies at New York University. Some of the ideas and concerns in these lectures have been tried out in one form or another in my seminars at NYU. I would not have been able to finish these lectures in time except for the help of my two graduate assistants, Christina Lombert of the Comparative Literature Department and Karim Abdul Mustapha of the Performance Studies Department. They combed all the libraries and bookshops of New York in search of materials and books that I urgently needed. The others before them, Marianella Belliard and Marylou Gramm, had also been very helpful when they contributed to the early phase of my research in these areas.

The ideas that make up these lectures have a history. The first, 'Art War with the State', has been developed over the years and I have given versions of it in Oslo and in Amherst, Massachusetts, and it formed the basis of the 1992 Dunning Trust Lecture at Queen's University, Kingston. The current version has gained from the reactions and comments of the previous audiences. Some of the ideas for the lecture had emerged during my preparations for one of my classes on literature and politics at Yale. I was reading Plato and suddenly found myself laughing loudly at his comments on art and society. They sounded very comical to me and they echoed so much of what had happened to me in post-colonial Kenya. Had the Kenyan authorities been reading the *Republic*? In the process I found myself revisiting Plato and Aristotle. I then became fascinated with Plato's use of myths and stories and dramatic settings for the unfolding of his arguments, hence my interest in the allegory of the cave, which formed the basis of my third lecture. The second, 'Enactments of Power', was inspired by a talk I gave to Professor Schechner's class on issues and methods in the Department of Performance Studies, Tisch, NYU, in the fall of 1995. I was in the midst of discussion on the performance of the past, drawing on my theatre work in Kenya when I realized that what I was really talking about was the politics of performance space. This linked well with the theme I had tried to explore in my seminar on performance in African prison narratives in the same department. The ideas in the fourth lecture have been developed at NYU, particularly in my classes on orature and contemporary African theatre in the Department of Performance Studies.

And lastly a note on the title. I have subtitled the lectures, 'a critical theory', because I am in part looking at the nature of orature, literature, language, performance, art, and the state, and their relationship. The term critical theory is here meant to echo a combination of literary and social thought and the notion of evaluation. Though I am grounding the theoretical exploration largely in Africa, the issues could apply wherever there are states, particularly post-colonial ones. But ultimately the complex tensions between social and imaginative powers, between the art of the state and the state of art, can only be suggested through images and hence the overall title: Penpoints, Gunpoints, and Dreams.

I am grateful for the support of my wife, Njeeri, and the entire family at Lima House, Orange, in the course of writing these lectures. I used the family circle to test some of the ideas I had for their titles, and I took into account their various comments and suggestions. And finally I want to thank Laurien Berkeley for her thorough and sensitive editing.

Ngũgĩ wa Thiong'o

New York University
July 1996

Contents

Introduction

I N August 1991 I visited South Africa, a guest of the Congress of South African Writers. My visit was in solidarity with the democratic forces in the sunset of the apartheid regime. In an interview with the BBC I was asked, how did it feel to be in South Africa at a time when I could not possibly go back to an independent Kenya? Indeed here I was, in a country where, until recently, writers had been gaoled, exiled, and murdered by the state; where the products of their imagination had often been banned; and where, at one time, my own works had been embargoed. Yet, here I was, speaking out as a guest of a progressive writers' organization without fearing that I would be gaoled, or worse, if I returned to my beloved country. I was the guest of a legally functioning writers' organization in what was, until recently, the world's leading republic of fear. But in my own country the Writers' Association of Kenya, of which I was the chairperson in 1982, had been completely crippled by the state. Most of the founding members of the association now live in exile.

Unfortunately what has happened to Kenyan writers is symptomatic of the general condition in contemporary Africa. As far back as 1967 Wole Soyinka, in a conference of African Scandinavian writers in Sweden, cautioned against complacency by writers in the then independent African countries, warning them that before very long they 'may begin to envy the South African the bleak immensity of his problems. For the South African has still the right to hope, and this prospect of a future yet uncompromised by his failure on his own part, in his own right, is something which has lately ceased to exist for other African writers.'[1] The recent execution of the Nigerian writer Ken Saro Wiwa by the Abacha military regime, in a country which has produced more writers than any other in the continent, brings out painfully not only the force and the truth of that prophetic warning but also the irony of contemporary African politics and arts. The deed was carried out against appeals for clemency by, among others, Nelson Mandela, now President of a free South Africa, but who had been in jail on Robben Island at the time of Soyinka's warning thirty years before. Writers are probably safer in South Africa than in any other part of the continent today. The execution also dramatizes the obvious fact that the writer in contemporary Africa had been seen as the enemy of the post-colonial state. His art is often regarded as an act of war against statesmen, a justification of the state's declaration of war against art and artists. The state's terror and paranoia about writing and writers is aptly summed up by the Egyptian writer Nawal el Sa'adawi in her *Memoirs from the Women's Prison*. Sa'adawi was gaoled by the Sadat regime in 1981. When a political prisoner asks for something with which to write, she is told: 'No pen and paper... that is utterly forbidden. Anything but pen and paper. Easier to give you a pistol than pen and paper.'[2] One day a warder, the *shawisha*, finds her writing on the ground with the tip of a little rock. 'One written word in a political cell is a more serious matter than having a pistol,' she tells Nawal. 'Writing is more dangerous than killing, doctor.'

The situation in Africa raises in turn the wider issues of the relationship between the art of the state and the state of art,

---

[1] Wole Soyinka, 'The Writer in a Modern African State', in Per Wastberg (ed.), *The Writer in Modern Africa* (Uppsala: Institute of African Studies, 1968), 15.

[2] Nawal el Sa'adawi, *Memoirs from the Women's Prison* (London: Women's Press, 1982), 49.

between rulers and writers, between Plato's guardians of the state and his mindless possessed who sing by the power divine. And this is what I want to explore in tonight's lecture and generally in the other three: the writer and the state, or more generally the artists and the guardians of a modern state. The first lecture, 'Art War with the State', contains also the general theme of the entire lecture series. There is a war going on between art and the state. Writing is more dangerous than killing, says the state. Even artists sometimes cast their role in terms of war. Mozambican anti-colonial poets used to talk about bullets beginning to flower. Nawal el Sa'adawi encounters a female prisoner who has been incarcerated because she killed her husband, whom she had caught in an incestuous relationship with her daughter, and the writer in Sa'adawi identifies with her:

I look at her strong brown fingers, and it occurs to me that they resemble my fingers. My heart beats as though with the same force which powers her heart. My eyes shine as if with the very same lightning sparkle. My hand as it grips the pen, is like her hand when she took hold of the hoe and struck the blow.

It is just as if I were striking blows with the pen at a corrupt, black head which wants to abduct my freedom and life, to deform my true self, and to force me to sell my mind and to say yes when I want to say no.[4]

The second lecture, 'Enactments of Power', will focus on the struggle between the artist and the state for the control of the performance space within and outside the national borders. Although I shall be drawing on my Kenyan experience, the issues go beyond the borders of Kenya. The third lecture, 'The Allegory of the Cave', will look at the role of the intellectual as an interpreter. I use Plato's allegory to examine the relationship between intellectuals, the state, and the control of psychic space in a post-colonial society. One way in which the state and the classes it represents exercise hegemonic control over the majority in colonial and post-colonial situations is through language,

[3] Ibid., 72.
[4] Ibid., 116.

and I shall also be touching upon the link between language policy and practice and issues of democracy and international relations. Can a people who have been denied the use of their languages effectively participate in the shaping of the country's destiny within the nation and between nations? The fourth lecture, 'Oral Power and Europhone Glory', will look at the irony of the African situation: that at the economic and cultural level, Africa produces, but the West disposes. In all four lectures I shall be examining how the state, particularly an autocratic state, tries to limit the ability of art to empower the people. Even where the state tries to use art as an ally, it is still suspicious of the reliability of that alliance.

Such a discussion inevitably brings to mind the famous dialogues in Plato's *Republic*, where Plato, in laying down the conditions under which artists could be admitted into his ideal state, sounds more like a comic employee of an autocratic post-colonial regime. His guardians, being founders of the state, may not themselves weave tales, for instance, but they ought to know the general forms in which poets should cast their tales and the limits which must be observed by them.

In fact engagement with classical Greece is one of the uniting themes in these lectures. This is not surprising. No student of English literature can have escaped studies of ancient Greece, and for an African student ancient Greece has particular fascination. It was basically an oral culture. As I will say in my fourth lecture, Socrates, for instance, would have been very much at home in many of the pre-colonial African societies. In fact, he would not have been executed for asking awkward questions since this is what was often expected of artists and Athamaki (Philosopher-leaders). Secondly, in culture, learning, and travel, classical Greece was more part of Africa than it was of barbarian Europe north of the Mediterranean. Certainly its connections with and borrowing from Egypt are no longer a matter of scholarly dispute. In one of his more daring leaps of comparative imagination, Professor Mazrui has speculated on the possibility of the Nile Valley civilization having been in part Ugandan and therefore East African. 'The point which needs to be grasped', he argues in the chapter 'Ancient Greece in African Thought' in his book *Political Values and the Educated Class in Africa*, 'is that Europe's title to the Greek heritage is fundamentally no different from Europe's title to Christianity. In these later phases of world history Europe has been the most effective bearer of both the Christian message and the Greek heritage. But just as it would be a mistake to let Europe nationalize Christianity, it would be a mistake to let her confiscate the hellenic inheritance. The Greeks must at last be allowed to emerge as what they really are—the fathers not of a European civilization but of a universal modernity.'[5] Although I use the term 'stolen legacies' in a slightly different context, my use of it is meant to echo that of George G. M. James in his book *Stolen Legacy*, one of the earliest systematic attempts to show the Egyptian basis and origins of Hellenic learning. Classical antiquity owed a lot to Africa through Egypt and the Nile Valley civilization and its East African connections.

These lectures, however, are not about ancient Greece. I am basically exploring the relationship between art and political power in society. I have always taken it that art is not outside the province of power struggles in society. But I have always refused to accept that art is something less than politics. When people ask me, why are you interested in politics, I always answer, because I am an artist. Whatever affects the lives of human beings, ecological, economic, political, social, cultural, or psychological, is within my province as a writer. I am not in art because of politics; I am in politics because of my artistic calling.

The other uniting theme is that of performance, both in the narrow sense of representation of an action as in theatre and in the broader sense of any action that assumes an audience during its actualization. The concept of performance is opening out new possibilities in the analysis of human behaviour, including literature. The exercise of power, for instance, involves variations on the performance theme. Performance distinguishes

[5] A. A. Mazrui, *Political Values and the Educated Class in Africa* (Berkeley and Los Angeles: University of California Press, 1978), 97.

political prison narratives from other narratives, including those
by 'non-political prisoners' or other narratives for that matter.
The prison is like a stage, but with the audience outside the
walls. Both the prisoner and the state are aware of this audience
and it explains some of the behaviour of the state and the artist-
prisoner. Some of this thinking can be found in the lecture
'Enactments of Power'.

In a world which is daily shrinking, the struggle for democratic space becomes very important. Space in the lectures is
used in a broad sense of territorial, temporal, social, and even
psychic. All peoples in all societies need more of this type of
space for creativity and self-expression. But the irony is that in an
age where science and technology have developed to a level
where it is possible to outlaw poverty, we see the return of the
Dickensian world on a global level. More and more people find
themselves confined to mega-ghettos. And the state, far from
being subject to social control of the majority, becomes even
more beholden to financiers. The credit-card mentality—based
on debt and mortgage of the future to satisfy the present—is
ruling the economies of the world. People see their languages
trodden down, their cultural and psychic space shrunken, and
their power to alter their social environment diminished. In such
a world, art, with its embodiment of notions of creativity and
freedom, needs to assert itself. It needs to be active, engaged,
insistent on being what it has always been, the embodiment of
dreams for a truly human world where the progress of any one
person is not dependent on the downfall of another; where the
health of any one person or group of people is not dependent on
the export of their leprosy to others; where millionaires are not
created on the backs of a million poor; where the state is so
subject to the social control of the majority as to wither as a
coercive power outside and above society. The goal of human
society is the reign of art on earth.

ONE

Art War with the State: Writers and Guardians of a Post-colonial Society

I

I N history the appearance of art in human life precedes the emergence of the state. There were body decorations, rock drawings, songs, and dances long before even the most rudimentary forms of the state. The state as we know it today has not always existed. As Engels argued in his book *The Origin of the Family and the State*, it is the result of the development of human society into antagonistic social strata. A power develops which stands above conflicting social interests, seemingly as a neutral force. Armed with coercive instruments and institutions, it regulates the whole society like a patriarch did his household in the feudal era. As late as nineteenth-century pre-colonial Africa, there were many communities which had not yet developed what Engels calls that 'special public power' above society which required taxes for its maintenance. This 'special public power' was largely introduced by colonialism to control and

keep the colonized in their place among the mines and plantations, and to tax them heavily to pay for various infrastructures
and for the maintenance of the military barracks, the police
cells, prisons, and the entire officialdom all the way from the
territorial governor to the lowest rung in the administrative
order. Before this, these societies, like the Ibos of Nigeria or
the Agĩkũyũ of Kenya, came close to Engels's self-acting armed
organization, in which everybody was everything: soldier,
farmer, counsellor, singer, priest.

One of the functions of the state is to ensure that the various
forces in society keep their place in the social fabric by policing
rules that are often codified into laws. In societies that did not
have a state, the function of holding together was carried out by
culture. The domain of culture embodied the desirable and the
undesirable in the realm of values. The values were contained in
stories, songs, and other cultural practices of the community.
Thus stories, dances, festivals, rituals, and even sports reinforced
each other in the production, reproduction, and dissemination
of ethical and moral ideals. In *Facing Mount Kenya*, Jomo Kenyatta describes, for instance, how the laws governing the stateless
Gĩkũyũ society were coded in dance movements.[1] And Okot
p'Bitek, in his book *Artist, the Ruler*, says that the artist uses his
voice to sing 'his laws to the accompaniment of the nanga, the
harp; he twists his body to the rhythm of the drums, to proclaim
his rules. He carves his moral standards on wood and stone, and
paints his colourful "do's and don'ts" on walls and canvas.[2] With

---

[1] Jomo Kenyatta, *Facing Mount Kenya* (New York: Vintage Books, 1965), 185–6.
This appears in a very interesting chapter on the Gĩkũyũ system of government.
After narrating the events of the revolutionary overthrow of autocracy, Kenyatta
describes the drafting of the new laws and regulations that would govern the
society. He adds: 'All the words of the drafted constitution were put into song-
phrases... It was considered that the most effective way of proclaiming the new
government was to call for war dances to be held in every district to give the
population an opportunity of hearing the announcement of the new constitution.
The suggestion was carried out unanimously for it was the only way through which
the words, phrases and rhythmic movements of the new songs and dances, in which
the laws and regulations of the new democratic government were embodied, could
be introduced effectively into the life of the community.'

[2] Okot p'Bitek, *Artist, the Ruler* (Nairobi: Heinemann, 1986), 40.

the rise of the state, the authority of a shared culture is replaced by the authority of a state. But it is not replaced altogether. The two authorities coexist. Okot p'Bitek argues that in every society there are two types of ruler: 'those who use physical force to subdue men, and those that employ beautiful things, sweet songs and funny stories, rhythm, shape, and colour, to keep individuals and society sane and flourishing'.[3] For the poet Shelley, artists were the legislators of the world, but unacknowledged, except of course in stateless societies, where art and culture reigned supreme. So both the state and the arts hold society together, and in that sense they have a common objective. There are other points of convergence. Writing and other verbal art forms, for instance, are rooted in words. The state is also rooted in words that make up the laws, whether written down or simply recited. The pen gives visible form to the words of a writer; the gun visible authority to the words of a ruler.

In every absolutist state the holder of the *pen*, which forces words on paper, is seen as the enemy of the holder of the *gun*, which enforces words of the law. Penpoints and gunpoints thus stand in confrontation. And yet the most easily noticed fact in looking at the artist and the ruler is the disparity in their powers: one has only a feather in his hand; the other, the entire killing machine behind him. One has the capacity to spill ink only, the other the capacity to draw blood. Why is the writer, or more broadly the artist, then, with his feather, with his bottle of ink, and a white piece of parchment, often seen as a threat to the absolutist state of whatever ideological colour, guise, or credo? Why do its rulers fear the open word, Brecht once asked in the poem 'The Anxieties of the Regime':

> Given the immense powers of the regime
> Its camps and torture cellars
> Its well fed policemen
> Its intimidated or corrupt judges
> Its card indexes and lists of suspended persons
> Which fill whole buildings to the roof

[3] Ibid.

> One would think they wouldn't have to
> Fear an open word from a simple man.[4]

Even in a democratic but class society the relationship between artist and ruler is still problematic and not without potential or actual conflicts. Part of the answer lies precisely in their very functions in society as two authorities, one moral, the other formal and legal, trying to legislate for the well-being of society. Are they genuine rivals for the allegiance of the community? Is there, in the very character of the state as a state and that of art as art, mutual antagonism? I will isolate at least four features of art which could illuminate the conflict and give a clue to why the creative state of art is always at war, actually or potentially, with the crafty art of the state. The four features have their opposite in the state as a state.

II

There is first of all a godlike aspect to art. The Gĩkũyũ word for the artist is *mũmbi*. It means the one who moulds, the creator. *Mũmbi wa Igũrũ na thĩ*: the creator of heaven and earth. That is the first artist. There is also *mũmbi wa nyũngũ*; maker of pots. One can go on and talk about *mũmbi wa mĩhianano*: maker of images. Plato in book 10 of the *Republic* talks of the makers of three versions of seemingly the same object, in his particular example, a bed: the original, in nature in its ideal essence, which is made by God; another, existing in nurture, which is made by a carpenter; and a third, existing as an image made by the painter. The Gĩkũyũ word covers the three senses: God, or nature; human labour, or nurture; and human imagination, or the image-making capacity of the human consciousness. Plato of course makes the distinction to disparage the third category of *mũmbi* as the furthest removed from reality, but in most cultures there has always been this association of creativity with divinity, with both human labour and human consciousness seen as

[4] Bertolt Brecht, *Poems* (London: Methuen, 1976), 297–8.

imitating God. The tree of knowledge from which the biblical Adam and Eve eat is really the tree of art, for only after they have eaten and are expelled from Paradise do they begin to make things and to experience the joys and pains of living and dying. We talk of a world made by people to contrast but also to parallel it with the world made by God. The connection is most obvious in comparing all the organic and non-organic substances in the universe and their imitative replication in the social environment—remember, for instance, how city lights look like heavenly stars when seen at night from the sky—and their imaginative correspondence in sculpture, paintings, and drawings. In music also: the universe is full of music, and human beings, in singing, could be seen as only imitating the choir of the heavenly spheres. But even in the realm of language there is a connection between God and the Word, for God, in nearly all cultures, originally manifests himself as the voice.

In the beginning was the Word, says the Old Testament, and the Word became flesh. The whole of Genesis is really a poetic celebration of the Word and its power. Let there be light; and behold, there was light. The Qur'an celebrates the same power: the words in it, in their very form and shape and arrangement, are supposed to have come directly from God. Language, its beauty, its power, its attraction, is behind the mesmerizing hold that all religions, particularly those with a written credo, have on the souls of their adherents. Even where there is no written sign, words and the sound forms of their oral articulation become even more important. Divinations, invocations, prayers of all kinds at their best are a pure feast of words. The mystery of Christianity used to be deepened by the use of Latin; and that of Islam, by the use of Arabic. The Agĩkũyũ people of Kenya believed that the voice of the singer of good words was really the voice of God.

The essence of both God and art is creativity. One brings different things together to realize a third, which may have some features of all those other elements but is certainly not identical to any one of them: it becomes a third particularity with its own individuality as an image, an object, or a living organism. The early Greek philosophers got it right when they thought of the entire universe as being composed of earth, air, fire, and water. Creativity is inconceivable without change. Change, the end-product of all creativity, is both an expression and the result of movement. In Epistle LXV, Seneca, of Roman antiquity, in his quest for the general cause of things, also discusses what he calls 'accessory causes'. It is interesting that to the five accessory causes—matter; agency; form; purpose; and idea, or pattern, which he identifies with Aristotle and Plato—he adds not only time and place but also motion, for 'nothing is either made or destroyed without motion. There is no art without motion, no change of any kind.' All these causes are only parts of the one efficient cause, divine reason—God—maker of the natural world, which is imitated by art through human reason. But it is clear that, for him, the essence of creativity is motion.[5] The essence of creativity is therefore motion. In this, the godlike aspect to art, lies the clue to the essential conflict between the state of art and the art of the state.

The state, like art, sees itself as a god, and especially in its ability to dispense death. In fact the state came into the world clothing itself with divinity; the sovereign was often said to be God's representative on earth. The aspect of godhood the state identifies with is not that of the creator of heaven and earth but that of the keeper of universal order, the one who holds every-thing in place. The state authorizes on earth what God authorizes in heaven. The state tries to hold together what is: its entire effort is to conserve and preserve society as it is. Laws and their enforcement are meant to make society function with a certain order. Stability is the key. It is interesting that in societies without states, God is less absolute and more human in his strengths and weaknesses. Among the Agĩkũyũ and the Maasai of Kenya, the other name for God is Ngai, the generous, giver, distributor, sharer. They also identify more with God as

---

[5] *Seneca in Ten Volumes* (Cambridge, Mass.: Harvard University Press; London: Heinemann, 1917), iv. 451.

mũmbi. But in societies with states, God tends to be more absolute in his authority and supremacy.

So a state, any state, is conservative by its very nature as a state. It wants things as they are, for it is constituted in the first place to ensure stability in a society with contending social forces and interests. Even in times of revolution the emerging state, after settling scores with the old regime and institutions, soon relaxes into safeguarding the gains and the new institutions from further changes. There is no state that can be in permanent revolution. Art, on the other hand, is revolutionary by its very nature as art. It is always revising itself—the avant-garde overthrowing old forms. Even in the work of the same artist there is a constant struggle to find new expression—a continual striving for self-renewal. And as for its relation to content, it looks at things not only as they are, but more essentially as they could be. Hence Aristotle's ancient observation in his *Poetics* that poetry is more universal than history, for the latter deals with things as they are, the former with things as they could be; in other words, with possibilities. Art strives towards perfection, the ideal union of form and content. But content is never still. It is constantly undergoing change. Art strives to capture the essence of reality, which is motion. It celebrates motion. Art is simultaneously stillness in motion and motion in stillness. The state strives towards the perfection of the form of things, such as the legal system, even where this is in conflict with a changing content. It wants to arrest motion, to continue with the repetition of the moment, supervise the known and the familiar. Stillness without motion: that is the essence of the art of the state.

Thus the notion of motion and change so central to art, thought, nature, life, is obviously in fundamental conflict with the notion of having arrived at the best of all possible worlds, the notion of finality, rest, which is death. Art is in opposition to Hegel's nineteenth-century talk of history as having travelled from East to the West, bypassing Africa of course, and finding its ideal realization in the Prussian state (how wrong he was anyway), or for that matter the talk of his twentieth-century counterpart Francis Fukuyama, with his proclamation, following the end of the Cold War and the collapse of communist states in eastern Europe, of the end of history in the liberal American state. We have arrived at the best of all possible worlds: thereafter it is matter of narration of the same liberal stability. 'What more could people want?' is a frequent phrase in the mouth of governors of the state. The notion of having arrived at perfection is very dangerous because it contains within it seeds of autocracy and intolerance. These are the latter-day echoes of the guardians of Plato's ideal republic, which has to be protected from artists, who might otherwise undermine its stability with the unregulated products of their madness.

The more absolutist and conservative a state is, the more it is likely to be hostile to any reminder of its social mortality. Art is always reminding the present of the obvious: even you shall come to pass away. A colonial state and a neo-colonial state, which are variants of an absolutist state, will inevitably come into conflict with any words and images that embody change. Absolute art is for the celebration of absolute motion, which is life: the absolute state is for the absolute cessation of motion, which is death.

III

Secondly, there is the Socratic aspect to art. You remember his story. A certain Chaerephon, his childhood friend, is told by the oracle at Delphi that there was no one wiser than Socrates. Instead of accepting the statement, Socrates sets about questioning people with the reputation of being wise, and he discovers that, whereas he is conscious of his ignorance, most of those with the reputation of being wise are not conscious of their ignorance and hence to the extent that Socrates accepts his ignorance and therefore seeks to know, he is wiser than the others: the wisest of people are those who realize, with respect to wisdom, that they are worthless. The effect of his questioning generates bitter hostility against himself. He is accused of crim-

inal meddling in that 'he inquires into things below the earth
and the sky and makes the weaker arguments defeat the
stronger'.[6] But note the actual charge in the deposition of his
accusers before the Athenian state: that he was guilty of corrupt-
ing the minds of the youth, and of believing in the deities of his
own making instead of those recognized by the state. In embark-
ing on the adventures of asking questions he was only following
the dictates of his conscience. In his defence, he compares
society to a large thoroughbred horse which because of its
size is inclined to be lazy and needs the stimulation of a
gadfly. 'It seems to me that God has attached me to this city
to perform the office of such a fly, and all along I never cease to
settle here, there, and everywhere, rousing, persuading, re-
proving every one of you.'[7] In practice he asks questions, and
for this he is eventually forced by the state to drink poison.
He died for the right to ask questions no matter how awkward;
and not, definitely not, for the right to have a monopoly
on answers, no matter how right and correct they may have
seemed to be. Despite his disparaging comments on poets and
performers, Socrates articulates the position of the artist in
society.

Art has more questions than it has answers. Art starts with a
position of not knowing and it seeks to know. Hence its explora-
tory character. In fact art has hardly any answers. There may be
answers implied in the questions. But they are often hints, open-
ended possibilities, and not certitudes. In that sense the questions of art are more akin to those of our daily greetings. We are
all familiar with those clichés of our daily interactions: 'How are
you?' 'What are you doing?' 'Where are you going?' The main
thing is that the answer is left to the recipient of the greetings.
The state, on the other hand, has plenty of answers and hardly
any questions. The more absolutist the state, the less it is likely
to ask questions of itself or entertain questioning by others. Like
those supposedly wise Athenians, who were so sure of their

[6] Plato, 'Socrates' Defence', in *The Collected Works of Plato*, ed. Hamilton (1994), 5.
[7] Ibid. 17.

wisdom that they were not willing to learn anything from Socrates, such a state has a narcissistic image of itself as the holder of absolute truth. In other words, absolute power is taken for absolute knowledge. Such a state regards those who ask questions as rebels, subversives, madmen.

The absurdity of a writer's situation when asking questions in a neo-colonial state or any variant of an absolutist state is best illustrated by the fate of my Gĩkũyũ-language novel *Matigari*, which came out in Kenya in 1986. Between 1982 and 1986 many writers and intellectuals were sent to prison or else forced into exile. The year 1986 was particularly bad for students and faculty. Even discussions in the university classrooms were often monitored by undercover police. It was in that climate that President Daniel Toroitich Arap Moi ordered the immediate arrest of the main character of my novel after intelligence reports had reached him of a person, Matigari, who was going about asking questions related to the truth and justice of what was going in the country. Actually Matigari was only asking one question: where could a person wearing the belt of peace find truth and justice in a post-colonial society? When the police found that Matigari was only a character in a novel of the same title good old Toroitich Arap Moi ordered the book to be apprehended instead. How dare a book ask questions? So in February 1987 in a very well co-ordinated police action, the book was taken down from all the shelves in all the bookshops and even from the publisher's warehouse. Art and literature are full of ironies, and what happened to the book in real life had already taken place inside the fictional world of the novel. At one point in the narrative, Matigari is arrested and put first in a police cell and later in a mental asylum, for only the politically deranged could ask the kind of questions he was posing to everyone he encountered. At another moment in the narrative Matigari is on the run, with the armed might of the state after him. More ironies: what happened to Matigari, the character, and *Matigari*, the novel, has happened to numerous Kenyan writers. The autocratic state does not have the humility implied even in the most ordinary of greetings. In 1969 the Kenyan writer Abdulatif

Abdalla was sent to prison for a leaflet that simply asked: *Kenya Twenda wapi?* 'Kenya, where are we heading?'

The Socratic aspect arises from the very nature of the artistic process as an exploration. We can define art as conscious dreaming in words, music, or colours. You know how our dreams at night sometimes yoke together the most incredible elements. For our dreams, nothing is sacred, that is beyond the bounds of its scrutiny as raw materials for its images. Even abstract notions like death and ghosts can take bodily form in the region of our dreams and nightmares. We get wings; we fly; we see ourselves die, get buried, and then wake up with gratitude for our waking life; we go to the gates of heaven or hell and back; we talk with the dead now resurrected and fully alive in our dreams. We hold money in our hands, we make love, even with our enemies, anything, and when we wake up we ask, in sweet remembrance or in terror; was I really flying? Crying? Was I really making love with So-and-so? And whether we like it or not, those questions force us to think about those things, to contemplate the ordinarily uncontemplatable. Each one of us has at one time or another used the sentence: 'Oh. I had such a dream' or 'I had such a nightmare', and of course we go ahead and tell it, or what we remember of it, wondering about the meaning of it all. The phenomenon and interpretation of dreams has intrigued humankind from time immemorial, including such actors in history as Aristotle, the biblical Joseph, and Messrs Freud and Jung. In his essay 'Daydreaming and Creative Writers', Freud links art with dreams. And Nietzsche, in his celebrated study *The Birth of Tragedy*, has explicitly linked the sources of art with the realm of dreams alongside that of intoxication. He quotes Hans Sachs as saying that 'all versifying and poeticizing is nothing but an interpretation of [dreams]'.[8] He adds: 'The beautiful appearance of the dream worlds, in creating which every man is a perfect artist, is the prerequisite of all plastic art . . . and of an important part in poetry also. In our dreams we delight in the immediate

[8] F. W. Nietzsche, *The Birth of Tragedy*, in *Philosophies of Beauty*, ed. Hofstadter and Kuhns (Chicago: University of Chicago Press, 1976), 499.

apprehension of form.'[9] The processes that trigger dreams as described by Freud in his *Interpretation of Dreams*, including the fact that many dreams draw on childhood experiences, are very similar to those which trigger the artistic imagination into flights of exploration. The difference between the images of our ordinary dreams and those of the dreams of art arise from the fact that one is a product of the subconscious of our interior senses, and the other, of a conscious process. It is like the conscious unlocking the subconscious and riding on the crest of imagination into every nook and cranny of our social, spiritual, and psychic being. The more the conscious is subsumed in the dream process, the more we feel the purity of the images; we do not stumble against an interfering authorial presence. Where is Shakespeare in all his plays? Which are his thoughts really? It was as if his plays came out of his system of imagination complete, Cleanth Brooks's 'well-wrought urn', so to speak. This is true of some of the best products of the human imagination in all cultures, especially in the stories of orature. They feel complete, almost effortless. Conscious dreaming, at its most intense where the conscious part, after triggering the subconscious, is itself almost totally subsumed by the dreaming process, is what Plato in *Ion* calls divine inspiration and possession. Such poets are under the influence of the Muses, like the Bacchic maidens who drew milk and honey from the rivers only under the influence of Dionysus:

For they tell us they bring songs from the honeyed mountains, culling them out of the gardens and dells of the muses; they, like bees winging their way from flower to flower. And this is true. For the poet is a light and winged and holy thing, and there is no invention in him until he has been inspired and he is out of his senses, and the mind is no longer in him: and when he has not attained to this state, he is powerless and is unable to utter the oracles. Many are the noble words in which the poets speak concerning the actions of men . . . for not by art does the poet sing but by the power divine.[10]

---

[9] F. W. Nietzsche, *The Birth of Tragedy*, in *Philosophies of Beauty*, ed. Hofstadter and Kuhns (Chicago: University of Chicago Press, 1976), 499.
[10] Plato, *Ion*, in *Philosophies of Beauty*, ed. Hofstadter and Kuhns, 55.

Although the passage underrates the power of reason, it is nevertheless a very lyrical rendering of the artistic process as inspiration. Plato's description is one of the origins of the association of artistic creativity with madness. For William Shakespeare the lunatic, the lover, and the poet are linked by the fact they all possess the power of imagination. Lovers and madmen in particular have such seething brains,

> Such shaping fantasies that apprehend
> More than cool reason comprehends.

It is these shaping fantasies which transform whatever is around into things of beauty or hell. But even the poet is possessed by the same 'shaping fantasies', for

> [His] eye, in a fine frenzy rolling,
> Doth glance from heaven to earth, from earth to heaven
> And, as imagination bodies forth
> The forms of things unknown, the poet's pen
> Turns them to shapes, and gives to airy nothing
> A local habitation and a place.[11]

But madness is when the dreaming process, the free association and yoking of images together, becomes uncontrollable by the conscious, even when a person is clearly awake. What connects conscious dreaming, subconscious dreaming, and the extremities of deranged minds is, however, the freedom to ask any questions even of the most taboo and sacred. A mad person, for instance, can utter anything, ask any questions, and even link different situations. And just as sane people are disturbed by the presence of a crazed mind, the state with its certitude is irritated by the uncontrollable character of dreams. Nevertheless, the artistic image differs significantly from the other types of dreaming and extremities of derangement, not only because it is a product of conscious dreaming—reason riding on the wings of imagination and powered by emotions—but because it also embodies the dreams of humankind for a more spiritually healthy existence. Any visions of a better life impose questions

---

[11] William Shakespeare, *A Midsummer Night's Dream*, v . i.

on the present order of things, and that was the Socratic dilemma. Questions can be a form of criticism, and this is as irritating to the state that thinks it knows everything as it was to those in Athenian Greece who thought they knew all there was to know. Thus art is a keeper of our dreams. A post-colonial state often crushes those dreams and turns people's lives into nightmares. In my novel *Matigari* there is a scene in which the fictional state issues a decree against dreams. Dreaming becomes a crime of thought and imagination.

IV

The Socratic aspect is allied to the first, godlike, aspect of art; but also to a third—what we shall call the Andersenian aspect. You all know the nineteenth-century Danish writer Hans Christian Andersen; his work has now become part of the human heritage. You will remember the story of the emperor's new clothes. You will remember how an entire people were ideologized into believing and swearing that the emperor was fully dressed— moreover in the most beautiful of clothes. It took the innocence of a child to say that the emperor was without clothes. He was naked, but nobody before the child's utterance had been willing to see it.

The Andersenian child was putting into words what his clear eyes could see, what was reflected in the mirrors of the camera in his head. In other words, his innocence was that of a mirror. Holding a mirror, what he saw reflected there was a naked head of state, and he said so. Again Plato in the *Republic*, while trying to disparage the works of imagination, brings out this mirroring element in art. The artist can become closer to the 'maker of all the works of all other workmen' by the simple process of turning a mirror round and round—'you would soon enough make the sun and the heavens, and the earth yourself, and other animals and plants... in the mirror'.[12] The artistic process is

---

[12] Plato, *Republic*, book 10, in *Philosophies of Beauty*, ed. Hofstadter and Kuhns, 31.

like a mirror lodged in the consciousness. It is a complex mirror with an X-ray element. It reflects whatever is before it—beauty spots, warts, and all—and it has even that capacity to mirror what is below the surface of things. So one way of thinking about art is that it is as Shakespeare's mirror unto nature, meaning that it reflects both the surface and the deeper nature of things. But we do not like all we see, even of ourselves, in the mirror.

Writers and their work do often carry the innocence of the Andersenian child. They even have the awkward habit of peering under the clothes of any emperor to see what could be hidden there. In indulging and following their imagination wherever it leads them, even to the realms of what could be, writers do often stumble upon truths, to which they give the bodily form of words. Thus the Andersenian child is also the great religious prophet, the founder of great religions, and the great scientific mind, who often has to flee to escape the wrath of absolute monarchs who think their kingdoms will come tumbling down at the words describing what the eye can see, the ear can hear, and the heart can feel. In this respect, Brecht's poem 'Anxieties of the Regime', which is about the rule of fear in Nazi Germany and the terror the rulers have of any word of truth even in the innocence of ordinary greetings, is very instructive. In the poem, Brecht compares the Third Reich to the house of Tar, the Assyrian, which according to legend was a mighty fortress which could not be taken by any army, but when one distinct word was spoken inside it, it fell to dust. Brecht could as well have been speaking about the 'word' in a colonial system.

What is so often forgotten is that the Nazi regime was simply one step on the ladder of the European colonial system. There is nothing that Hitler did which had not been done to Africans by European nations since the Renaissance. A colonial state, like the Nazi regime of Brechtian description, is built on a structure of lies. It is a system of violent subjugation of one people by another. But economic and political subjugation is often given rational legitimacy through an elaborate education and philosophic system. This can range from the crudest type of racist reductionism about the superior and inferior natural endowments of the victimizer and the victim in that order to the more sophisticated type about higher cultures, languages, and values, to which the elect from among the inferior could eventually be adopted and consequently attain a semblance of equality. All the racist myths so well documented by Aimé Césaire in *Discourse on Colonialism*, Eric Williams in *Capitalism and Slavery*, C. L. R. James in *The Black Jacobins*, and by many other writers from Asia, Africa, and South America were meant to obscure the elaborate system of lies. A neo-colonial system, equally, is erected on a structure of lies, for it acts as if it is free and independent while it is essentially a continuation of the hated colonial system by other even more pernicious means. But note that even within a fairly independent national state, a whole web of lies is often woven to justify the subjugation of the majority by a minority. Rulers of colonial, neo-colonial, and authoritarian states take to the extreme the position of Plato's guardians of the state that 'if any one at all is to have the privilege of lying, the rulers of the state should be the people; and they, in their dealings either with enemies or with their own citizens, may be allowed to lie for the public good'. The problem with an autocratic state, or any variant of an absolutist state, is that it often regards its own citizens as enemies anyway, and the rulers often lie for their personal good and security. Such a state would fear words of truth even if they came from the mouths of unarmed babes. The whole point about Brecht's poem 'Anxieties of the Regime' is that those who rule by fear end up being ruled by fear:

> Driven by anxiety
> They break into homes and search the lavatories
> And it is anxiety
> That makes them burn whole libraries. Thus
> Fear rules not those who are ruled, but
> The rulers too.[13]

---

[13] Brecht, *Poems*, 297.

The South African apartheid regime used to ban books, music even, which described what had actually been witnessed in the streets by television cameras. It did not happen, said the regime. The same was true of colonial and now also of post-colonial Kenya. In 1990 Kenyan musicians were arrested for making music about the state's killings of the urban dwellers of Muoroto in Nairobi: it did not happen, said the Moi regime, despite the fact that these deaths had been witnessed by local and international journalists and clerics. From 1992 to the present the same regime dresses a special killer squad of its paramilitary police force as 'tribesmen' in order to commit massacres in the Rift Valley Province against members of other communities. This squad acts out 'tribal' warfare. In the urban areas the same squad acts out gang warfare against the opposition forces. 'It did not happen,' says the regime, despite eyewitness accounts, reports from the dominant churches, and condemnation by international human rights organizations. The same fear of the word of truth from the Andersenian child goes to the extent of the regime's trying to remove the word and the event from history and memory.

The reaction of the state to the truth of the Andersenian child sometimes takes the form of discrediting what has been seen, to make the child and those who heard the word begin to doubt— can you really believe a child?—or forget what had taken place— do you really believe that an emperor could be naked? There is a devastating description of this process of the state trying to rub out facts from history and memory in Gabriel García Márquez's novel *A Hundred Years of Solitude*. About 3,000 striking workers are massacred in the banana-republic phase of the fictional Macondo. But 'the official version repeated a thousand times and mangled out all over the country by every means of communications the government found at hand, was finally accepted: there were no dead'.[14] Of course those who insisted on talking about it have been hounded into eternal silence by the military. To the relatives who witnessed the extermination

---

[14] Gabriel García Márquez, *A Hundred Years of Solitude*, (Picador, 1978), 252.

the army would insist, 'You must have been dreaming... Nothing has happened in Macondo, nothing has ever happened, and nothing will ever happen. This is a happy town.'[15] Even those who were present at the massacre begin to doubt if they have really seen it. State historians begin to immortalize the government version. Years later, the very few who talk about the massacre sound as if they are all talking about something that never really happened, as if they are telling a 'hallucinated version because it was radically opposed to the false one that historians had created and consecrated in the school books'.[16] George Lamming, in his novel In the Castle of My Skin, tells of a similar erasure of the memory of slavery in African children through the education system. The Andersenian child begins to doubt if he has ever seen the emperor really naked. But the truth is immortalized in Márquez's narrative A Hundred Years of Solitude, and in George Lamming's In the Castle of My Skin, and in that sense the fictional texts play the role of the Andersenian child who gives words to what everyone has seen but is too blinded by the authority of the state to voice.

V

This brings me to the fourth aspect. It has something to do with the voice and I shall name it in a while. Here I am using 'the voice' in its broadest possible sense: both in the Priscianite sense of a combination of utterances articulated and non-articulated, scriptible and non-scriptible; and in the Augustinian sense of the sign, the various things that point to a reality not identical with themselves as the sign. I am thinking of the broadest possible human gesture expressing a meaning, a wish, a judgement, a mood, a situation of being. The state and the arts struggle for the voice of the community: one to silence it and the other to give it to silence.

[15] Gabriel García Márquez, A Hundred Years of Solitude, (Picador, 1978), 252.
[16] Ibid. 283.

The Ethiopian writer Hama Tuma illustrates very well this side of a repressive post-colonial regime in his collection of short stories *The Case of the Socialist Witchdoctor*. In the tradition of great satirists, Hama gives us narrative sketches of life in Ethiopia both under Emperor Haile Selassie, and under the Dergue, the military regime that overthrew him. In one of the stories, 'The Case of the Traitorous Alphabet', Doch Melke, a worker for a government printer for thirty years, is arraigned in court because one issue of the official newspaper, *Rally*, has come out with the word *Tidkem* spelt *Tikdem*, which would make the sacred slogan *Ethiopia Tidkem*, 'Ethiopia First', read *Ethiopia Tikdem*, meaning 'Ethiopia Weak'. He is sentenced for life to cleaning toilets in the government press. He is also sentenced to undergo the sisyphean task of continually setting up print which will be disassembled the moment he finishes. As the narrator comments wryly, in times of revolution the first victims are words. But in his fictional Ethiopia the revolution has murdered the alphabet. 'What do you expect?' he asks. 'We are poor and we can't afford even words!'[17] In the title story 'The Case of the Socialist Witchdoctor', another Ethiopian intellectual is accused of practising counter-revolutionary witchcraft. Actually all he does is make people, particularly government officials, face up to their hypocrisy as a way of cleansing the sickness within them. He is of course found guilty and is sentenced to life imprisonment, during which 'the accused is to be kept totally silent. No one shall talk to him and he will be punished severely for every word he utters. He shall burn in his own thoughts and unspoken words.'[18]

But art tries to restore voices to the land. It tries to give voice back to the silenced. Imagine the silence of words in their materiality on paper. Imagine the apparent silence of sculpture. But you can hear their voices. Even a piece of sculpture can scream. Perhaps we should call this aspect of art the Munchian aspect. Edvard Munch was a Norwegian painter. You remember

---

[17] Hama Tuma, *The Case of the Socialist Witchdoctor* (Oxford: Heinemann, 1993), 73.

[18] Ibid. 52.

those orangy colours on his canvas? He painted the famous screaming figure. No matter how you look at it, it screams, it screams loud and clear. Even when one has gotten away from it, it continues to scream through the silence in the temple of one's mind. It is screaming silence across both time and space. The scream is well illustrated in the soft voice of a gourd in a story by Okot p'Bitek. Okot p'Bitek was a Ugandan writer who called his long poems Songs. In his songs, as in his life, Okot was like the Socratic gadfly, raising many awkward questions which quite often irritated those in power and the entire African middle class, which likes to identify with Europe against Africa. Okot p'Bitek was also a great storyteller. And the fourth aspect of art, the aspect that links him to the Munchian screaming figure, is contained in one of the stories he used to tell. The story is now in a collection of his narratives called *Hare and Hornbill*, but the story itself is called 'Hare and his Mother in Law'.

Hare is generally a trickster figure in orature. He is to East Africa what Spider is to West Africa. He functions best as a symbol of the weak outsmarting the strong. But he is also tricked by those who are even weaker, like ants or even plants. The story goes that Hare marries a beautiful girl but finds that his mother-in-law is even more beautiful. Hare plans to make love to his mother-in-law, but without anybody ever finding out, because such an act is incestuous and a matter of great shame. Hare studies the habits of his mother-in-law and notices that every day when the sun is at a certain point in the sky, not too hot, sending out just the right warmth, Mother-in-law always goes out in the yard and sits in one spot. Hare digs a hole and buries himself inside it. When Mother-in-law comes out to sun herself she discovers that the sun is particularly warm that day. The scene is repeated for a couple of days and Hare is very happy about it. Mother-in-law is enjoying the sunshine; Hare is enjoying himself; and, more importantly, nobody sees or catches them in the act. He is fooling everybody. Unfortunately, there is one silent observer to the whole thing. A gourd. A gourd has no speech. It is a silent presence. Like a work of art. A painting, a sculpture, any work of art hanging on the wall is seemingly silent when ignored by those around it. The gourd is silent in the same way. Or so Hare thinks. In the evening, when everybody is around the fireside, the gourd starts singing that Hare has done something very sweet with his mother-in-law. But Hare does not let the gourd finish the story. Hare throws the gourd out in the yard. But there it starts singing even louder. Hare follows it out, crushes it to small bits, grinds it, and swallows it. He is back among company, satisfied that he had silenced the gourd for ever. But his stomach begins to rumble and the voice begins. Hare rushes out and shits out the whole mess. The seeds grow, the gourd plants roots, it begins to multiply, and now its song cannot be silenced. The complicity between Hare and Mother-in-law is exposed in the song of the gourd. The truth is finally out! The Okotian story, and in particular the song of the gourd, is a metaphoric confirmation of the Munchian aspect to art: even silence can speak in the service of truth. And truth can only empower the people.

A neo-colonial state tries to impose silence on the population as a whole. Quite often the right to organize has been taken away. People are not allowed to gather freely to voice their thoughts. At one time in Kenya, Toroitich Arap Moi tried to ban discussions of politics on public transport. Another decree tried to stop music being played in cars and on public transport. In such a situation, you can see how the state of art will inevitably clash with the art of the state. A novel, or any narrative, may create a situation in which people are debating the very issues forbidden in real life by the state. The narrative in its very existence, and in the voices represented within it, are actually breaking the code of silence. The novel in nineteenth-century Russia gave voice to the tsarist-imposed silence on the majority poor. That is why Lenin, reviewing the works of Tolstoy, described him as the mirror of the Russian revolution. Because in Tolstoy's work the peasants had found their own voice.

Art gives voice to silence in the great prophetic tradition. Socrates was only voicing doubts that were in the hearts of those who were silent. The Andersenian child was only voicing what everybody could actually see but remained silent about.

Writers in contemporary Africa are saying what the majority can
actually see but about which they remain in enforced silence. It
is this capacity of art as a voice of silence that is behind the
Wordsworthian comment about that which was often thought
but ne'er so well expressed. Joseph Conrad said that what he was
trying to achieve by the power of the written word was 'to make
you hear, to make you feel,—it is, before all, to make you see'.[19]
Art was only making people more intensely aware of that which
was already there. In the process, art arms silence with voices
that, even when the bodies that carry them are crushed and
ground to powder, will rise again, and multiply, and sing out
their presence, as in the case of the gourd in Okot's story. Art in
this sense is silence that screams.

VI

It would seem to me, taking all the four aspects of art and their
opposites in the state into account, that the state, when functioning to its logical conclusion as the state, and art functioning
as art are antagonistic. They are continuously at war. The state
in a class society is an instrument of control in the hands of
whatever is the dominant social force. Art, on the other hand, in
its beginnings was always an ally of the human search for freedom from hostile nature and nurture. But this conflict inherent
in the two may not always be visible because the state does not
always act with a sledge-hammer against all artistic creations and
representations. In the complexities of history and social forma-
tions, the state and the arts do not always function in their
logical absolutes. Artists, after all, are products of social classes
and ranks, and their imagination takes flight weighed down by
ideological moorings consciously or unconsciously held. Edward
Said has rightly cautioned against the position that authors 'are
mechanically determined by ideology, class, or economic history', but he also makes the apt observation that, nevertheless,

[19] Joseph Conrad, 'Preface', *The Nigger of the Narcissus* (Penguin Books, 1963), p. 13.

they 'are in the history of their societies, shaping and shaped by
that history and their social experience in different measure'.[20]
This applies to all artists. In moments of evolutionary and
revolutionary changes, when a new society is being born out
of the womb of the old, artists may even come to feel and act as
if they and their works are allies of the emerging states and the
new social order they promise. In his book *The Meaning
of Literature*, Timothy Reiss has made a persuasive case that
there was precisely such an alliance of literature and power in
seventeenth-century western Europe, principally in France, England, and Spain; that many writers saw themselves as allies of the
emerging political order. Arts and Arms were often in accord in
its creation and rationalization. 'Literature was a servant—
indeed, an integral part—of political order and might, an instrument for the maintenance, after the creation, of a particular
society and its values.'[21] Reiss cites, among several others, the
interesting case of Cardinal Richelieu, who in 1635, less than a
year after he took France into the Thirty Years War, founded the
Académie française with the express purpose of making the
French language perfect, elegant, and able to treat all arts and
sciences. Reiss comments: 'Richelieu was clear that the language
and *belles-lettres* of France were to be suitable tools serving a new
kind of centralized national authority and bureaucratized mon-
archy.'[22] This was a period of more or less evolutionary, though
profound, changes in seventeenth-century Europe. Equally,
twentieth-century African literature written in European languages emerged in a period of profound changes and certainly
it saw itself as part of the anti-colonial nationalism, and hence
the spirit of optimism, in much the pre-independence literature.
Similarly, following the Russian Revolution of 1917 many writers
saw themselves as part of the emerging workers' state. In such
moments art may be remembering its own past, when, in its
pre-state and pre-class being, it was the voice, the dominant

[20] Edward Said, *Culture and Imperialism* (New York: Alfred Knopf, 1993), p. xxii.
[21] Timothy J. Reiss, *The Meaning of Literature* (Ithaca, NY: Cornell University
Press, 1992), 149.
[22] Ibid. 72.

moral legislator, of the entire community. In any case, those moments are often pregnant with possibilities, and the emerging state appears as if it is the harbinger of a new tomorrow. In such situations art and the state may see themselves reflected in each other, fellow travellers so to speak, even if it is a matter of time before they part ways, as Timothy Reiss argues happened to European literature after the seventeenth century. The state would like it better if the arts and artists became its willing allies. In fact more often than not it will try to find ways of exercising control over the demons of imagination. Let me isolate five principal ways in which the state has tried to react to the collective power of the four aspects of art.

It will try to appropriate the magic power of art through co-option of artists either because the artists themselves come from and are sympathetic to the social stratum in power, or because the state is buying their services outright. In time it may even come to have a corpus who will work within the general forms and limitations set up by the guardians of the state. These will try to produce an art that seems to negate the notion of change and hence is flattering to the believers in the eternal stability of the present. Or they may produce artistic objects that try actually to embody the didactic and ideological needs of the state. But, even more importantly, they will produce an art that does not show the guardians of the state in a negative light à la recommendations of Plato in the *Republic*. In his state, remember, Plato will admit only those artists who will not show the gods and kings in negative lights, for instance by describing their quarrels amongst themselves or their exhibitions of coarse behaviour. The state may in fact raise to positions of honour those who promise to make their mirrors reflect only the desired image. At the very least the state will try to give its implicit or explicit blessing to the art that gives the faintest of voices to silence and anoint it as the desirable model. But if art was able to do all the above, it would negate itself as art. The mirror, even a bad mirror, may be focused on the intended object, but it is surprising how often it will reflect other objects around and which might make those viewing the scene see more into it than they were intended to do. A mirror that did not reflect would negate itself as a mirror. That is why even the most consciously intended didactic elements in art are often negated by the mirror effects and character of art. Or the observer may see in the very intended image another meaning all together. The more realistic the reflection, even within the narrow focus, the more the realism will make the observer aware of the silences surrounding the image. Intellectuals with historical experience of colonialism and anti-colonial resistance can read the Western canon with clarity and new insights in part because their culture of struggle has prepared them to see the implications of certain commissions and omissions, but also because the texts themselves contain the possibilities of such alternative readings. The material for the brilliant interpretations of such as Ahmed Iqbal and Edward Said was already in the texts, but it had never been so well brought out and so succinctly expressed. Edward Said can see a great artist in Rudyard Kipling although 'few more imperialist and reactionary than he',[23] because Kipling's realism could bring out the contradictions in imperialism, often undermining his very avowal of allegiance to that imperialism and reaction. Said argues that in *Kim* Kipling rendered India with great skill, and the novel 'not only depended on a long history of Anglo-Indian perspective, but also, in spite of itself, forecast the untenability of that perspective in its insistence on the belief that the Indian reality required, indeed beseeched, British tutelage more or less indefinitely'.[24] This comment captures well the capacity of art to reflect, refract, and re-evaluate reality. The truth of art, and that of Kipling's conscious belief in and commitment to the British state, were really at war in the same text. One of the positive sides of deconstruction aesthetics is the way it makes one look at omissions, evasions, and echoes in literary images.

If the co-option of artists fails the state may ban the actual works, and this has been the norm in colonial and post-colonial states, and apartheid South Africa. Otherwise the state may try

[23] Said, *Culture and Imperialism*, p. xxi.
[24] Ibid., p. xxi.

censorship almost as if it is taking a leaf out of Plato's *Republic*: '[The] thing will be to establish a censorship of the writers of fiction, and let the censors receive any tale of fiction which is good, and reject the bad; and we will desire mothers and nurses to tell their children only authorized ones only. Let them fashion the mind with such tales, even more fondly than they would the body with their hands.'[25] In censorship the state tries to control the distribution and consumption of the work of art. But when official censorship fails, the state may try to induce self-censorship through selective acts of terrorism.

In some countries, the state can be very clever and actually kill the power of art though taming it. Equally applicable to art is what Lenin once said of the fate of revolutionary theory in bourgeois society in his book *State and Revolution*:

During the lifetime of great revolutionaries, the oppressing classes constantly hounded them, received their theories with the most savage of malice, the most unscrupulous campaigns of lies and slander. After their death, attempts are made to convert them to harmless icons, to canonize them, so to say, and to hallow their names to a certain extent for the 'consolation' of the oppressed classes and with the object of duping the latter, while at the same time robbing the revolutionary edge and vulgarizing it.[26]

Literary products do not have to await the death of the authors: they are quite often turned into harmless icons even in the lifetime of the artist. The opposite of creating icons is also possible: to ignore the writer all together. This is related to what one might call the Cassandra aspect of art. Cassandra is the slave-girl in Aesychlus' *Agamemnon*, the first play in the cycle of Orestes, who had the gift of prophecy but was fated never to be believed. In such a situation the state does not see any threat to itself from the voices of the condemned. The Western state has been the most adept at this kind of game. The post-colonial state is too impatient, too unsure of itself, and hence too

---

[25] Plato, *Republic*, book 2, in *Philosophies of Beauty*, ed. Hofstadter and Kuhns, 9.
[26] V. I. Lenin, *State and Revolution*, (Moscow: Progress Publishers, 1965).

intolerant to kill art by turning it into a national icon or by ignoring its prophecies.

There is of course a fourth possibility: the reconciliation of art and the state by having artists as heads of state like Plato's celebrated philosopher-kings. In Africa we have had two writers as heads of state: Sédar Senghor, one of the premier poets of negritude, the first president of Senegal: and Augustino Neto, Angola's first president, who was one of the leading poets in Africa. In the Czech Republic we now have in Václav Havel a successful playwright as president. In such a situation, the person is wearing two basically irreconcilable hats. As the head of state he can only adopt the tolerant position of live and let live. Otherwise, should the state become more repressive, he could be forced to suppress even his own work, depending on its mirroring power and clarity and the extent to which it gives voice to the silence of the majority against the state of which he is the current embodiment. Sédar Senghor once banned one of Sembene Ousmane's films, *Ceddo*, under the pretext of a literary disagreement about the spelling of the word 'Ceddo'; Senghor wanted it spelt with one 'd'. The story is told of how the late Eric Williams, independent Trinidad's first prime minister, banned his own book *Capitalism and Slavery* because its main thesis went against the ethics of the neo-colonial capitalist economy to which he was now committed. I do not personally know if the story is true—and the book is not the work of imagination—but, whether true or not, it expresses very well the impossibility of reconciliation between art and the state in a class-structured society. It would be impossible for a Sédar Senghor or a Václav Havel to write very powerful works in the defence of the state, let alone a repressive one. Art is more powerful when working as an ally of the powerless than it is when allied to repression. For its essential nature is freedom, while that of the state is the restriction and regulation of freedom.

And yet it is this very power that makes the state want to co-opt art into its service. For in trying to co-opt, silence, censor their works, turn them into harmless icons or try reconciliation by unifying state and art in the body of one individual, the artist-king, the state is actually acknowledging its power. And for all their disparaging tone and comments about poets, Plato's dialogues contain some of the most pertinent observations on the sources and power of art. To paraphrase what Blake said of Milton and *Paradise Lost*, Plato was on the side of the artistic devil without knowing it.

When the state has failed in its four stratagems for the containment of art, it tries to exercise complete control over the artist in two principal ways. The first is to maim his mind and body. Many prison narratives are really tales of the state's attempts to break the mind of the artist by isolating it from whatever ordinarily feeds it. Imprisonment is a way of isolating the artist from the experiences of daily living which feed his imagination. And in prison, the state takes away books and other intellectually stimulating materials from him or else allows him only the heavily censored. The state also tries to control the means of literary production. If the state does dish out pen and paper to a political artist-prisoner, it is with the hope that it will make the captive write down a guilty plea, or an apology, or simply put his signature to a state-manufactured confession. The author, on the other hand, tries to outwit the prison authorities in order to get hold of the means to write his own accusatory messages. In his prison notes *The Man Died*, Wole Soyinka best dramatizes this struggle for the means of literary production in an incident in which he pickpockets the prison doctor to secure a pen. In addition the state may well attempt to maim other organs of the body that writes. In the story, *The Case of a Presumptuous Novelist*, Hama Tuma tells how the military regime imposes silence on a novelist who writes love-stories instead of praises to the revolution. This is done by the very expedient act of amputating the offending hands that hold the pen. As the Prosecutor proclaims: 'You can't punish a seditious writer properly unless you cut his hands off.'[27] In other words, torture, physical torture, is frequently used to coerce the artist into total submission.

---

[27] Tuma, *The Case of the Socialist Witchdoctor*, 115.

The other way is to expel the artist from his society altogether through exile or death. Exile has become the occupational hazard of the writer and thinker in history. Even Aristotle had to escape from Athens, arguing that he would not let the city offend twice against philosophy. All histories of world literature, from biblical times to the present, have their stories of writers and prophets in exile. Colonial and post-colonial Africa are no different, and I doubt if there is a single country in our continent which is free of this stigma. But the ultimate guarantee of final control and silence is death. Again there are many sad cases of fine artists, from apartheid South Africa to Idi Amin's Uganda, for instance, who have lost their lives. The execution of Ken Saro Wiwa in Nigeria is the latest in this dastardly saga. There is also the case of Salman Rushdie, who is daily stalked by a death sentence which could be carried out by any one among the millions of Muslim believers. His case is even more striking in the sense that his offence is against not one but several states.

Prison, exile, and even death have something in common: they are acts of removing the artist from the territorial stage, leaving the state as the sole performer of power. So although they are extreme consequences of the struggle between art and the state, they are also the result of a general attempt by the state to control performance in general and the performance space in particular. We shall see this in the next lecture, when I talk about the performance of power and the power of performance and the struggle for the control of the performance space.

TWO

Enactments of Power: The Politics of Performance Space

I

T HE struggle between the arts and the state can best
be seen in performance in general and in the battle
over performance space in particular. Performance
is representation of being, the coming to be, and the ceasing
to be of processes in nature, human society, and thought.
If before the emergence of the state the domain of culture
embodied the desirable and the undesirable in the realm
of values, this was expressed through performance. The
community learnt and passed on its moral codes and aesthetic
judgements through narratives, dances, theatre, rituals, music,
games, and sports. With the emergence of the state, the artist
and the state became not only rivals in articulating the
laws, moral or formal, that regulate life in society, but also
rivals in determining the manner and circumstances of their
delivery.

This is best expressed in Plato's dialogue the *Laws*. The
Athenian describes how, as the representatives of the state,

they must respond should the tragic poets come to their city and ask for permission to perform:

We will say to them, we also according to our ability are tragic poets, and our tragedy is the best and noblest; for our whole state is an imitation of the best and noblest life; which we affirm to be indeed the very truth of tragedy. You are poets and we are poets, both makers of the same strain, rivals and antagonists in the noblest of dramas, which true law can alone perfect, as our hope is. Do not then suppose that we shall all in a moment allow you to erect your stage in the agora, or introduce the fair voices of your actors, speaking above our own, and permit you to harangue our women and children, and the common people, about our own institutions, in language other than our own, and very often the opposite of our own.[1]

The war between art and the state is really a struggle between the power of performance in the arts and the performance of power by the state—in short, enactments of power. The conflict in the enactments of power is sharper where the state is externally imposed, a situation of the conqueror and the conquered for instance, as in colonialism.

Jomo Kenyatta dramatizes this confrontation in *Facing Mount Kenya*. The story goes that there was a brief period of kingship in Agĩkũyũ society. This was replaced by a new, more egalitarian system rooted in the family as the basic unit. The replacement was effected through a revolution, *ituĩka*, which literally means a break, a complete break with what has gone before. The new revolutionary councils, all the way up to the highest co-ordinating body of elders, derived their authority from below. The coming-to-be of this new system was celebrated through a ceremony called Ituĩka every twenty-five years or so. The ceremony also marked the passing of power from one generation to another. The festival was spread over a period of six months and involved the entire land inhabited by the Agĩkũyũ. Thirty years after the British colonial state was established in about 1895 the Agĩkũyũ community was involved in a flurry of activities to

---

[1] Plato, *Laws*, book 7, in Hofstadter and Kuhns (eds.), *Philosophies of Beauty* (Chicago: University of Chicago Press, 1976), 52.

celebrate the Ituĩka ceremony, but this was stopped by the colonial state. The performance of Ituĩka was taken as a challenge to its power. The annual parade of British military might at the opening of the new sessions of the legislative assembly replaced *ituĩka*-type performances.

The main ingredients of performance are space, content, audience, and the goal, whose end, so to speak, could be instruction or pleasure, or a combination of both—in short, some sort of reformative effects on the audience. The state has its areas of performance; so has the artist. While the state performs power, the power of the artist is solely in the performance. The state and the artist may have different conceptions of space, content, goals of performance, either of their own or of the other, but they have the audience as their common target. Again the struggle may take the form of the state's intervention in the content of the artist's work, which goes by the name of censorship, but the main arena of struggle is the performance space—its definition, delimitation, and regulation.

II

'I can take any empty space and call it a bare stage,' says Peter Brook in the opening line of his book *The Empty Space*. A man walks across the empty space while someone else is watching him, and this is all that is needed for an act of theatre. I want to pose the question: is a performance site ever empty as in the title of Peter Brook's book?

There are many ways of looking at performance space. One is to see it as a self-contained field of internal relations: the interplay between actors and props and light and shadows—the *mise-en-scène*—and between the *mise-en-scène* as a whole and the audience. The outer boundaries of this space are defined by a wall, material or immaterial. The material could be stone or wood or natural hedges. The immaterial is the outline formed by the audience in what is otherwise an open space. The director utilizes the entire playing-field, *ithaakīro*, to maximum effect on both the actors and the audience. He will look for various levels, heights, centres, and directions of force in the acting area. But these levels and centres acquire their real power only in relationship to the audience. The entire space becomes a magnetic field of tensions and conflicts. It is eventually transformed into a sphere of power revolving around its own axis like a planet in outer space. This is the real magic and power of performance. It incorporates the architectural space of material or immaterial walls into itself and becomes a magic sphere made still by its own motion, but it is potentially explosive, or rather, it is poised to explode. That is why the state, a repressive machine, often targets its nervous eyes on this aspect of the performance space. For even if it does not explode, might it not, by its sheer energy, through its laser-beams of power, ignite other fields? For the magic sphere is not suspended in total isolation. There are other social centres and fields of human actions: farms, factories, residences, schools. Life goes on there, births, marriages, deaths, and their representations in celebratory festivals of welcome or in dirges of farewell.

Which brings us to another way, the second way, of looking at performance space. The performance space is also constituted by the totality of its external relations to these other centres and fields. Where are they all located relative to each other? Who accesses these centres and how frequently? It matters, in other words, whether, say, the artist's space is located in a working-class district, in a bourgeois residential neighbourhood, in the ghettos, or in the glossy sections of our cities. The real politics of the performance space may well lie in the field of its external relations; in its actual or potential conflictual engagement with all the other shrines of power, and in particular, with the forces which hold the key to those shrines. The shrines could be the synagogue, the church, the mosque, the temple, parliament, lawcourts, television and radio stations, the electronic and print media, the classroom, playing-fields of all sorts and guises. In other words, it is often not so much a question of what happens or could happen on the stage at any one time, but rather the control of continuous access and contact.

These questions of access and contact become very pertinent in a colonial and post-colonial state, where the dominant social stratum is often not sure of its hegemonic control, and particularly where the population is divided not only on the traditional lines of the urban and the rural but also on racial and ethnic fissures. And within those run class divisions. The gap between the poor and the rich is so glaring, so immediate, and so visible, that the state may want to get rid of the performance spaces which keep on chafing this area of friction. In such a situation, the question whether the space should be inside a building or not may acquire a deep symbolic value and become the site of intense power struggles.

And thirdly, the performance space, in its entirety of internal and external factors, may be seen in its relationship to time, in terms, that is, of what has gone before—history—and what could follow—the future. What memories does the space carry and what longings might it generate?

It is clear from this that the performance space is never empty. Bare, yes; open, yes; but never empty. It is always the site of physical, social, and psychic forces in society. It is the instinctive awareness of this which prompts the Athenian in Plato's *Laws* never to want to permit the serious performing artist to harangue women, children, common people about 'our institutions'. And hence the battles over performance space.

Drawing concretely on my own experiences in theatre in Kenya, and on specific productions, I want to look at the performance space of the artist. Then I shall briefly look at the state's own areas of performance, and finally at their interactions and consequences on the body and mind of the artist and the population as a whole. We shall see that the politics of post-colonial performance space is a complex interplay of the entire field of internal and external relations of these forces in the context of geography, time, and history.

III

First the space of the artist. That this space, however bare it looks, is not empty came home to me when in 1976 I became involved in the production of the play *The Trial of Dedan Kīmathi*, whose national and world première was in Nairobi on 20 October that year. The script was a joint effort by Mīcere Mūgo and me. We were then colleagues in the Literature Department of the University of Nairobi. Although she and I had for a long time discussed the possibility of collaborating on a play, it is ironic that what actually triggered intensified efforts on our part was a call by the state. The venue for the Second World Black and African Festival of Arts and Culture originally scheduled for Zaïre had been changed to Lagos, Nigeria, for February 1977. Kenya would be represented in all the events from displays of material culture to performing arts, including theatre.

With the representation of Kenya in Lagos in mind, the Ministry of Social Services, under which culture and cultural institutions were administered, had set up a national committee to oversee all the preparations. This in turn set up subcommittees for the various events. The Drama Subcommittee was given the task of coming up with two plays. I was initially the chairman of this subcommittee, but later, when the play in which I had collaborated with Mīcere Mūgo was submitted for consideration, I gave up the chair, and Seth Adagala took up the position. Seth Adagala then worked with the Ministry, having resigned, a few years before, as the first and then the only African director of the Kenya National Theatre. The Drama Subcommittee eventually selected two plays, *The Trial of Dedan Kīmathi* and *Betrayal in the City* by Francis Imbuga. The two plays were to be run under the name Kenya Festac 77 Drama Group. Tirus Gathwe was to direct *Betrayed in the City* and Seth Adagala, *The Trial of Dedan Kīmathi*. As chairman of the Ministry's subcommittee, Seth Adagala was to be in overall charge.

In June 1976 the Festac 77 Drama Group came up with a brilliant but really common-sense proposal: since the two plays were supposedly going to represent Kenya in Lagos, it was important that they were performed first to audiences in Kenya, as a matter not of privilege but of right and necessity. There was an added reason: Kenya was going to host a Unesco general conference; there would be many delegates from all over the world, and it would do Kenya's image a world of good were the delegates to see effective African theatre. The question now was simply one of the best 'symbolic' time and venue.

The month of October was finally selected for two reasons. The Unesco meeting was to be held that month. But October was also the month in which Kenyans celebrated the heroes of anti-colonial struggles. We were also unanimous on the question of the venue: the Kenya National Theatre. After all it was called National; and it was under the Ministry of Social Services; and surely, apart from anything else, it would be the focal point for the Unesco delegates. Guardians of international education and culture, they would surely be interested in what the Kenya National Theatre would offer during their stay in the country. Thinking that everybody would applaud this, the leadership of the Festac 77 Drama Group presented the proposals to the management of the National Theatre. We were sure that there would be no problems: logic and good sense pointed to the selected time and place.

The first wake-up call took us all by surprise. The management, which was almost entirely composed of Europeans linked to the major European amateur and semi-professional groups, told us that there was no room in the inn! But this was in 1976, thirteen years after formal independence under the presidency of Jomo Kenyatta. We drew their attention to the symbolism of the event; the dignity of Kenya before the world; the fact that Kenyans needed to see the play before Lagos; and surely apart from anything else Kenyans needed to remind themselves that their independence was won through sweat and blood and the deaths of many. No room in the inn. The management was already committed to Bossman's *Jeune Ballet de France* and the City Players' *A Funny Thing Happened on the Way to the Forum*. At this crucial moment and in a national venue, Kenya would be seen through the eyes of a French ballet and a British farce.

In the course of the struggle over dates and venues there now arose basic questions of principle. Shouldn't the Kenya National Theatre and the Kenya Cultural Centre be catering primarily for national interests? In planning for cultural activities over the year, did the management not take into account the Kenyan image inside and outside the country? What shows should be performed on national days? And for the eyes of the world like the forthcoming Unesco conference? So many questions, so few answers, except that, for us, there was simply no room.

The management argued that the dates had been booked months before; that African plays never attracted theatre-lovers anyway. Statistics were even quoted as evidence. They had never stopped to ask why, even assuming their allegations to be true, there had always been a low turn-out of Africans at the theatre. Were the reasons not very evident in what they were proposing to offer as Kenyan culture before the eyes of the world in October? Could it not be that over the years the National Theatre had created the image of a service station for Western shows like *Godspell, The Boyfriend, The King and I, Jesus Christ Superstar*? Or more truthfully a service centre for the kind of theatre described as deadly in Peter Brook's book?

Actually behind the conflicting positions and arguments were deeper questions of the performance of history. The story of the space defined as national theatre was intertwined with that of the subject-matter of *The Trial of Dedan Kīmathi*, and that of the entire country. Three stories locked together in the unfolding drama of times and venues.

The National Theatre complex was actually constructed by the colonial state. According to Richard Frost, former head of the Empire Information Services and the British Council's first representative in East Africa, the theatre had been put up under direct instructions from the Colonial Office to meet the urgent needs of good race relations in the colony through cultural practices. The National Theatre and the Cultural Centre complex were to be a place where 'people of culture and position' could meet. In the book *Race Against Time*, Frost elaborates on this thus:

At that time no Africans were able to live anywhere near the site which was selected, but the site was selected because it was hoped that in due time the residential apartheid would be brought to an end and Muthaiga, Westlands, the Hill and other areas, which were then open only for Europeans, would become districts where leading people of all races would live. As it was not to be a 'working-class' theatre, it was built in the middle of the 'well-to-do' Nairobi.[2]

The National Theatre space was also going to be the host site of the Kenya Schools Drama Festival. The British Council, which had hatched the scheme in 1951, had hoped to 'win the goodwill of Europeans and to help them keep at a high standard the cultural heritage of Britain'. Theatre was the perfect instrument:

Drama was a cultural activity enjoyed by both actors and audiences and it was also an activity in which Africans and Asians engaged. It was hoped that through the theatre the goodwill of the European community could be gained, and, later on, members of the different races could be brought together by participation in a common pursuit which they all enjoyed.[3]

So, right from the start, the place had been seen as an empty space on which a predominantly British theatre was going to help in the construction of a new chapter of good race relations in the country.

But the site was not a space empty of history and in which, now, a narrative of new race relations could be written through the mediating eyes of the Colonial Office in alliance with a colonized people of goodwill. Next to the National Theatre site was, and still is, the Norfolk Hotel, built by Lord Delamere, one of the early British settlers, at the turn of the century. It was in fact known more popularly among the settlers as the House of Lords because that was where the colonial white nobility, or pretenders to nobility, used to meet for drinks and gossip and politics. The Norfolk Hotel overlooks the site where in 1922 African workers were massacred by the British police. The workers were marching to the central police station to demand the

[2] Richard Frost, *Race Against Time* (London: Rex Collings 1975), 73.
[3] Ibid. 196.

release of their leader, Harry Thuku, who had been arrested and later imprisoned for eight years because of his involvement in the nascent workers' movement. Their march was interrupted by gunfire from the police. The police were also joined in the massacre by the white lords on the terraces of the Norfolk Hotel. The figures of the dead are in dispute. The British admit to twenty-two only; but there were at least 150 dead. The bodies of the dead and wounded lay sprawled on the ground on the site which years later was to house the National Theatre complex and the University of Nairobi. Harry Thuku became a nationalist hero, the subject of many songs and dances. But opposed to Harry Thuku and his workers' politics were the colonial-appointed chiefs who had even founded the first ever loyalist movement in the country. The colonial state and the loyalist chiefs were on the same side in blaming the massacre on the victims.

The massacre had also attracted international protest. Marcus Garvey, on behalf of the Universal Negro Improvement Association, dispatched a telegram of protest to the British prime minister Lloyd George, in which, *inter alia*, he said: 'You have shot down a defenceless people in their own native land exercising their rights as men. Such a policy will aggravate the many historic injustices heaped upon a race that will one day be placed in a position to truly defend itself not with mere sticks, clubs and stones, but with modern implements of science.'[4] Garvey's prophecy came true in 1952 when a 22-year-old former primary school teacher and accountant escaped the tight security net and slipped into the mountains to become the most formidable leader of the Mau Mau armed guerrilla forces. His name was Dedan Kīmathi.

Under his leadership the Mau Mau guerrillas put up one of the most heroic struggles against imperialism in the twentieth century. It is often forgotten that while liberation movements in places such as Guinea-Bissau, Mozambique, Angola, and Algeria

---

[4] Quoted in Ngũgĩ, *Detained: A Writer's Prison Diary* (London: Heinemann, 1987), 40.

had free neighbouring territories which served as rear bases, Mau Mau guerrillas were completely surrounded by the enemy administration. They had to depend almost entirely on what arms they could steal from the enemy forces and what they could make in the underground arms factories in the country's cities and forests. Before Kimathi's capture in 1956 and execution in 1957, even the British government and the colonial state had to admit that, despite thousands of soldiers brought from the British bases all over the world, and despite bombings on a scale reminiscent of the Second World War, there were virtually two governing authorities in Kenya: the colonial authority led by the Governor and Mau Mau, led by Dedan Kĩmathi.

The period saw the most incredible upsurge of Kenyan culture. It was a general grass-root-based performance of hope. There were several newspapers in Kenyan languages. Songs and dances celebrating the African past, condemning colonial practices, and calling for freedom had erupted. In the educational field, people had developed their own schools under the Kikuyu Independence Schools Movement and Kikuyu Karĩng's Schools Association. This educational movement culminated in the building by the people themselves of the first ever institute of higher learning in the country under the name Gĩthũngũri African Teachers' College, led by Mbiyũ wa Koinange, a Columbia University graduate. The symbolic importance of this can be seen in the fact that not until 1960, three years before Independence, was the second institute of higher learning, the University College of Nairobi, built, ironically on a site next to both the Norfolk Hotel and the National Theatre.

The colonial state retaliated. In October 1952 a state of emergency was declared. African-run schools were closed down because they were seen as performance sites for the nationalist forces. Gĩthũngũri Teachers' College was closed as an educational institution and the building turned into a prison where captured Mau Mau guerrillas and sympathizers were hanged. All cultural performances were stopped. And on 20 October 1952 Kenyatta and hundreds of leaders of KAU, the Kenya African Union, and of Mau Mau, were arrested. Kenyatta and seven

others were later tried in what became one of the most celebrated trials in colonial history, now immortalized in the book
by Montague Slater *The Trial of Jomo Kenyatta*. The defendants
were found guilty of leading Mau Mau and were imprisoned for
eight years with hard labour. The colonial state did not bother
with the trials of hundreds of others; they were summarily sent
to concentration camps all over the country.

The play *The Trial of Dedan Kīmathi* tries to capture that
heroism and the determination of the people in that most
glorious chapter of their history, not only a moment that helped
to break the back of the British Empire and its entire colonial
policy, but also, for Kenyans, a moment that was the culmination
of all the previous struggles waged by the other resistance heroes
of our history such as Waiyaki, Me Katilili, and Koitalel. Kīmathi
saw himself in the tradition of that struggle, but also in that of
the Peasants' Revolt in Britain, an event he referred to in a letter
addressed to the British from his hide-out in the mountains. The
play tries to capture the fears and the hopes, the promises and
the betrayals, with hints that history could repeat itself.

It is now evident that both the venue and the time—the days
and the month of October—carried different memories. For the
management, 1952 was the year the National Theatre was constructed and opened. And between 1952—the year that saw the
declaration of a state of emergency, the banning of independent
African performances, and the outbreak of the Mau Mau armed
struggle—and 1963—the year of formal independence—the
National Theatre space had remained a site for basically British
theatre into which Africans could be admitted as they matured
into people of culture and position.

It was these men and women of culture and position who
after Independence were indeed able to integrate into those
special areas that Frost talks about: Muthaiga, Westlands, and
the Hill. Independence removed racial apartheid but retained
economic barriers. Some of these African Kenyans defined by
the British as men of culture and position were also to assume
very important seats in the new post-colonial government. One
of these was Charles Njonjo, the son of one of the early colonial

chiefs who were part of the loyalist movement opposed to the nationalist politics of Harry Thuku. He became Attorney-General and, as a patron of one of the European performing groups and with his social linkage to most of the members of the management of the Kenya National Theatre and Cultural Centre, he was to play a crucial role in ensuring the uninterrupted control of the space by men and women who could maintain standards already set by the colonial state. And for him, although he himself was a black African, the only people who could ensure that continuity were British white. In other words, colonial practices were to be the yardstick for performative culture at the space. It was not surprising, therefore, that the management of the Centre could sincerely feel they were doing their duty to Kenya by staging a French ballet during the historically significant month of October and during a Unesco conference hosted by Kenya. For them the symbols of French ballet and a British farce stood for the authentic tradition of an Anglican Kenya.

The Trial of Dedan Kīmathi stood for a different tradition. It was celebrating the Mau Mau heroism and its centrality in bringing about independence for Kenya. But even more importantly, it was linking itself to the culture and aesthetic of resistance developed by the Mau Mau activists as they fought in the mountains, as they resisted in prison and concentration camps and villages, and as they called for a new Kenya and a new Africa. A good number of these songs and dances, now available in a collection of Mau Mau patriotic songs edited by Maina Wa Kīnyattī under the title *Thunder from the Mountains*, were incorporated in both the text and the performance of the play.

So the conflict over the performance space was also a struggle over what cultural symbols and activities represented the new Kenya. The country had emerged from an anti-colonial struggle: could a colonial culture and heritage effectively form the basis of its nationhood and identity? Even small acts could carry conflicting visions of the new Kenya. At a time when the Festac 77 Drama Group was trying to carry out a performance that reflected national history and to devise emblems that symbolized this, the management of the Kenyan National Theatre were selling Christmas cards of the National Theatre building as it was in 1952. It was then of course flying the Union Jack, the British flag, and this was quite prominent on the cards.

                                    IV

The Ministry, probably embarrassed by press notices that a Kenyan play had been handcuffed on Kenyatta Day, intervened, and the Festac 77 Drama Group was given eight days between 20 and 30 October to use the space. So in effect the two plays, *The Trial of Dedan Kīmathi* and *Betrayal in the City*, were crammed into four nights each between Bossman's *Jeune Ballet de France* (10 to 18 October) and the City Players' *A Funny Thing Happened on the Way to the Forum* (1 to 21 November). That in effect meant that the two European shows would take up a total of thirty-one days to our eight.

Despite this, the success of the two productions was astounding, especially in terms of the reception by African audiences. Every single one of the eight nights was sold out. The opening night of *The Trial* was particularly memorable because Kīmathi's wife and children were prominent guests, and they later stayed with the cast almost the night long telling stories of the war and singing many of the songs over and over again. As one newspaper put it, 'never before has the story of Kenya's freedom struggle been told with such force and conviction'. Nor, if I might add, had any previous production at the National Theatre been received with so much enthusiasm by a Kenyan audience. For those eight nights, the space had been truly nationalized by the feet of so many from all walks of life who came on foot, in private cars, and in hired vehicles to sing and dance with the actors.

But the dramatic highlight still belongs to the opening night. As the actors sang their last song and dance, through the middle aisle of the auditorium, they were joined by the audience. They went outside the theatre building still dancing. What had been confined to the stage had now spilled out into the open air and there was no longer any distinction between actors and the audience. It became a procession, and they weaved their way towards the historic Norfolk Hotel, towards the terraces from where in 1922 the settlers had helped the police in their mas-sacre. Even in 1976 it was still largely patronized by whites, mostly tourists. As the procession was about to cross the road, they were met by a contingent of police, who now told them, politely but firmly, to turn back. There was no antagonistic physical confrontation. The actors danced back to the National Theatre, formed a circle outside, and continued with their dances and songs, which talked about all the heroes of Kenyan resistance. The scene outside the theatre building continued every night of the four days allocated to *The Trial*, but the attempt to dance onto the premises of the Norfolk Hotel was not repeated. Nevertheless, it was as if the cast and the audience were trying to create an open space all around the Kenya National Theatre building, a space which would allow them to communicate better with the spirits of those who had died in 1922. A name which kept on cropping up in the singing was that of Mary Mūthoni Nyanjirū, the woman who led the workers' procession and the first to fall under the hail of colonial bullets.

After the eight days allocated to the two plays, we all vacated the space, peacefully. The Europeans came with their produc-tions. One day Seth Adagala and I were summoned to the Nairobi Headquarters of the Criminal Investigation Department for a few questions about performances at the theatre—actually, one question: why were we interfering with European perfor-mances at the National Theatre? The only possible 'interference' we could think of was the very success of our venture. No charges were filed against us, but there was an implied threat in the fact of the police summons and questions.

V

For some of us it was clear from that experience that, if Kenyan theatre was ever to thrive, it would have to find and define its own space in terms of both physical location and language. *The Trial of Dedan Kīmathi* had been staged in English in a controversial location. The real national theatre surely lay where the majority of the people resided: in the villages in the countryside and in the poor urban areas. It would have to be the site of a combination of what Peter Brook describes as holy theatre, rough theatre, and immediate theatre. It would have to be a theatre that went to the root of the historical space of the people's experience in order to speak to their immediate presence as they faced their tomorrow. To achieve any of that, it was important, we felt, to have a performance space directly under the control of the people. Those are some of the concerns that led to the foundation of the Kamĩrĩĩthũ Community Education and Cultural Centre.

I have told bits and pieces of Kamĩrĩĩthũ's story in three of my books, *Detained: A Writer's Prison Diary*, *Decolonizing the Mind*, and *Barrel of a Pen*, so I shall not go into too many details here. The project which was started in 1976—a literacy and cultural programme with theatre at the centre—became a truly community affair involving peasants and factory and plantation workers then resident in the village of the same name. In 1977, together with the community of this village about thirty kilometres from the capital, Nairobi, we developed a play, *Ngaahika Ndeenda* 'I Will Marry When I Want', in which people sang songs about their own history. Here were peasants and workers who only the year before were illiterate, who were used to singing songs of praise about the leadership and what it had done for the people, but who now could not only read and write but were actually singing with pride about their own abilities, what they had done in history, and now their hopes of what they could do tomorrow. What is more, they had built an open-air theatre in the centre of the village by their own efforts, and with no hand-outs from the state. They had reclaimed their historical space.

They tried to do the same when in 1982 they attempted another play, *Mother Sing for Me*. Again it was pride in their own history and faith in their own abilities, and hence their hope for the future, which was important. Professor Ingrid Bjorkman, who did research on Kamĩrĩĩthũ, has written a book that really testifies to this aspect. She came to Kenya in 1982 in the after-math of the government repression and interviewed the actors and members of the audience who had come to see the play in the public rehearsals before the ban. She closes her main text with the words of one of those who had attended the show:

The remarkable thing is that in our kind of system it is believed that we have people who have to think for us. As workers and peasants, people who actually toil, we are not supposed to use our heads. And you are not supposed to be mentally productive. You are not supposed to associate things and see a picture. You are always supposed to see things in isolation and you always know that you are being led into anything. Now here Ngũgĩ showed in Mother Sing for Me that peasants can think and they can communicate those thoughts—the understand-ing of their environment to other people. They can understand what makes them that which they are. It beats somebody, who has always known that he is a thinker, to think that a peasant could act and could also form songs that could express himself. . . . So this feeling that the peasants can understand a situation and actually communicate what they are thinking is what became the biggest threat. Because to be led you have to be 'sheep'. And when you show that you are not 'sheep', the leader becomes disturbed.[5]

The attempt to locate theatre among the people would raise new questions and answers about the content, form, and lan-guage of African theatre. But in November 1976 I did not realize that the attempt to locate culture where it belonged would raise even more problems and questions, not only about the perfor-mance space of the artist but about that of the state as well to the consideration of which we now turn.

VI

'All the world's a stage', said Shakespeare in As You Like It, 'And all the men and women merely players; They have their exits and their entrances.' The nation state sees the entire territory as

---

[5] Ingrid Bjorkman, 'Mother Sing for Me': People's Theatre in Kenya (London: Zed, 1989), 97.

its performance area; it organizes the space as a huge enclosure, with definite places of entrances and exits. These exits and entrances are manned by companies of workers they call immigration officials. The borders are manned by armed guards to keep away invaders; but it is also to confine the population within a certain territory. The nation state performs its own being hourly, through its daily exercise of power over the exits and entrances, by means of passports and visas and flags.

Within that territorial enclosure, it creates others, the most prominent being prison, with its entrances and exits guarded by armed might. How did prison, a much narrower stage, come to be such an important site for the state's performance of punishment? The state would prefer to act out its power, watched by an audience over the entire territory. In the television age, this is possible, though there are restraints. Historically, punishments were not always enacted in a hidden enclosure. In *Discipline and Punish*, Foucault has described in minute detail scenes of punishment in eighteenth-century Europe very much in terms of spectacle—what he calls the theatrical representation of pain by the state. 'There were even some cases of an almost theatrical reproduction of the crime in the execution of the guilty man—with the same instruments, the same gestures.'[6] These used to happen in the open. 'In the ceremonies', writes Foucault, 'the main character was the people, whose real and immediate presence was required for the performance. An execution that was known to be taking place, but which did so in secret, would scarcely have had any meaning. The aim was to make an example, not only by making people aware that the slightest offence was likely to be punished, but by arousing feelings of terror by the spectacle of power letting its anger fall upon the guilty person'.[7]

In his article 'Theater for an Angry God', Mark Fearnow has described a similar phenomenon in eighteenth-century America. He talks of the public burnings and hangings in colonial New York in 1741 in terms of performance—what he describes as the

---

[6] Michel Foucault, *Discipline and Punish* (New York: Vintage, 1979), 45.
[7] Ibid. 57–8.

most revolting ends to which theatrical techniques can be applied: 'public execution as popular entertainment, the display of rotting and exploding corpses as triumphant spectacle'.[8] But this spectacle did not always produce the desired ends, particularly on the audience. The condemned, by his reaction to the pain, could sometimes win the sympathy and even the admiration of those watching, and there was always the danger of the crowd intervening. The people drawn to a spectacle that was meant to terrorize them could express their rejection of this punitive power and sometimes revolt. 'Preventing an execution that was regarded as unjust, snatching a condemned man from the hands of the executioner, obtaining his pardon by force, possibly pursuing and assaulting the executioners, in any case abusing the judges and causing an uproar against the sentence— all this formed part of popular practices that invested, traversed and often overturned the ritual of public execution.'[9] And even after his death the so-called criminal could turn into a saint and come back to haunt the state. The condemned found himself transformed into a hero by the sheer weight of the drama and publicity surrounding his case. 'Against the law, against the rich, the powerful, the magistrates, the constabulary, or the watch, against taxes and their collectors, he appeared to have waged a struggle with which one all too easily identified.'[10]

There were precedents before the eighteenth century. The most famous case in biblical antiquity is that of Jesus Christ, whose public execution was later to haunt the Roman state and empire. So in time this open-air theatrical representation of pain was withdrawn from the open space into an enclosure. But, wryly comments Foucault, 'Whatever the part played by feelings of humanity for the condemned in the abandonment of the liturgy of the public executions, there was, in any case, on the part of the state power, a political fear of the effects of these ambiguous rituals.'[11]

[8] TDR (Theater Drama Review), T150 (Summer 1996), 16.
[9] Foucault, Discipline and Punish, 59–60.
[10] Ibid. 67.   [11] Ibid. 65.

Fearnow describes the same fear—the threat to public order in the fairs that developed spontaneously around such executions—as being what lay behind the banning of the gibbet in England in 1845. The truth of these observations is attested by real historical cases as described by Foucault, but also in literature. The Dickensian condemned man could always win sympathy, even if only that of a small boy like Pip for the Magwitches of the world. In Kenya the colonial state tried public executions and displays of bodies of the Mau Mau condemned, but this always aroused more anger against the state, as I have dramatized in my novel *A Grain of Wheat*. And when in 1984 the post-colonial state ordered processions to watch my effigy being burned and the ashes thrown into rivers, lakes, and the ocean, the spectacle only aroused more sympathy for me and the cause I was espousing: the release of all political prisoners in Kenya. Although the practice of public punishment still continues in some countries, and certainly in other more indirect ways throughout the world, removing the spectacle of punishment from the larger territorial space into an enclosure becomes a logical development. No state wants its designated criminals transformed into heroes and saints, with the possibility of their graves becoming some kind of revolutionary shrine.

But though the punishment was removed from the open into an enclosure, the element of performance remained particularly so for political and intellectual prisoners—artists, mostly. The prison yard is like a stage where everything, including movement, is directed and choreographed by the state. The *mise-en-scène*, the play of light and shadows, the timing and regulation of actions—even of eating and sleeping and defecating—are directed by armed stage-hands they call prison warders. It is a proscenium stage with the fourth wall added and securely locked so that there is no question of a privileged spectator peeping through it and seeing the action. Nevertheless, both the state and the condemned artist are aware that there is an interested audience outside the walls of the enclosure. The state tries to interpret, for the audience outside, what is happening inside the closed walls: the prisoner has confessed, the prisoner is healthy, or whatever fabrications it wants to feed the world.

The prisoner tries to counter the government propaganda by whatever means are at his disposal. Escape is impossible, suicidal even. So he resorts to pen and paper when he can find them. Hence the struggle for the literary means of production that I alluded to in my last lecture. Prison narratives by artist-prisoners are essentially a documentation of the battle of texts and of the continuing contest over the performance space of the state. This contest, while aimed at the groups of interested watchers outside the gates—Amnesty International, International Pen, and other human rights groups—is ultimately aimed at the real audience: the people waiting in the territorial space. The state is trying to direct the drama of the prisoner's self-condemnation—a confession of crimes of thought, his own guilt so to speak—and this has parallels with the gallows speeches of medieval and feudal Europe: 'The rite of execution was so arranged that the condemned man would himself proclaim his guilt by the *amende honorable* that he spoke, by the placard he displayed and also by the statements that he was no doubt forced to make. Furthermore, at the moment of execution, it seems that he was given another opportunity to speak, not to proclaim his innocence but to acknowledge his crime and the justice of his conviction.'[12] The artist-prisoner resists in every fibre of his being displaying 'the placard of self-condemnation', and even if he is forced, through torture, to display it, he will try to dispatch to the world, through some of the more sympathetic stage-hands, another placard denying the content of the first. This contest over the prison performance space of the state is also a means of resistance, a means of staying alive in this torture-chamber of the spirit. It is, in other words, one of the ways of denying the state a triumphant epilogue to its performance.

---

[12] Foucault, *Discipline and Punish*.

VII

There is no performance without a goal. The prison is the enclosure in which the state organizes the use of space and time in such a way as to achieve what Foucault calls 'docile bodies' and hence docile minds. The struggle for subjugation of the mind of the artist-prisoner is paramount. That is why once again books and reading materials become such vital objects of struggle. Prison narratives are full of incidents about books that one is not allowed to read and those one can read. The authorized and banned list, a kind of index of the prison inquisition, can be an insight into the mind of the state. In his book *Kenya: A Prison Notebook*, historian Maina wa Kĩnyattĩ records many episodes in which he is not allowed to read any of my works. Ngũgĩ's novels are political, they are dangerous, he is told over and over again during his six and a half years in various maximum-security prisons. But he has to find ways of reading these books, or similar ones, and Maina wa Kĩnyattĩ is amused by the fact that he can read Richard Wright and Maxim Gorky without problems. A political prisoner in fact is acting out an aesthetic of resistance through bodily or mental gestures. He is fighting against the intended docility of the mind. Even within the prison walls he will try to create a physical, social, and mental space for himself. He will try to use his allotted time and space and his limited social interactions in a manner that gives him maximum psychic space.

We have a humorous illustration of this in Hama Tuma's *The Case of the Socialist Witchdoctor*. In the story 'The Case of the Prison-Monger', Hama Tuma tells of an Ethiopian intellectual who describes himself as a prison maniac. He claims that he really loves prison. Every time he comes out of prison, he commits a crime, however petty, so that he can be sent back to gaol. The prosecuting team asks him, 'Doesn't it bother you to spend ten years of the prime of your life behind prison walls?' 'No', he replies. He argues that people are really in prison only when they believe themselves to be so. A house can be a prison. Even a palace can be a gilded prison for a king. On the other hand, the monk who shuts himself up in total isolation in a cave is not in prison. 'In prison, I met very many really free people', he asserts to the utter astonishment of the judge-prosecutor, who cannot understand this logic. Then follows this exchange:

What sentence do you now expect for your crime?
I should be sent to prison for five years as article 689 of the penal code states.
What if you are set free?
That will be a crime, the accused says really shocked at the possibility of freedom.
But if you are set free, would you commit a crime again?
I couldn't avoid it. For the public good and mine.
If you commit three more crimes, you will be killed.
Then death will be a relief indeed. Not punishment but real salvation.[13]

And now comes the judgement:

You, the accused, you are a no-good, fast-talking, lazy, strange, crazy person. You are a parasite. You are also dangerous. Whoever finds joy in prison, whoever feels free in our jails goes against the order of things, goes against the expected. A cow can't give birth to a puppy. Prison is a punishment, not a source of calm and freedom. If such feelings as yours spread, our security will be in chaos. I agree with the prosecutor. You are hereby sentenced to immediate freedom.[14]

The accused almost faints with shock at his sentence. When he recovers, he is shouting and screaming at the judge, 'You can't do this! You must send me back to prison!' The point is now made. For him the actual prison, the enclosure, is less evil than the wider territorial space under the military regime. The entire country is one vast prison where people's movements are tightly controlled, where they can be dislocated from familiar spaces into those easily patrolled. In any case, dislocation and dispersal can be one way of removing any basis of a collective performance of identity and resistance. The method had been tried during plantation slavery in America and the Caribbean islands.

[13] Hama Tuma, *The Case of the Socialist Witchdoctor* (London: Heinemann, 1993), 120–1.
[14] Ibid. 121.

VIII

In *Song of Ocol*, by Okot p'Bitek, the leading character, a member of the post-colonial ruling élite, actually wants to ban all performance so that they may not reflect his blackness. He wails, 'Mother, mother, why was I born black?' But the easiest way is to obliterate the rural space altogether, because this is the site of those performances that most remind him of his African being. His vision for post-colonial Africa is in terms of a huge city that swallows the rural completely:

> I see the great gate
> Of the city flung open
> I see men and women walking in.[15]

The rural person has only two alternatives:

> Either you come in
> Through the city gate
> Or take the rope
> And hang yourself.[16]

Do we hear in this echoes of English economic history with its enclosures in the eighteenth century? The goal is to take away the land which is the basis of the peasantry and turn the tillers into wage-slaves in the urban enclosures called factories and ghettos. It is another way of restricting the performance space of the tiller.

Prison then is a metaphor for the post-colonial space, for even in a country where there are no military regimes, the vast majority can be described as being condemned to conditions of perpetual physical, social, and psychic confinement. The state performs its rituals of power not only by being able to control exits and entrances into the territorial space, its entire performance space, but also by being able to move people between the various enclosures within the national territorial space. But the

---

[15] Okot p'Bitek, *Song of Ocol* (Nairobi: Heinemann, 1988), 149.
[16] Ibid.

aesthetic of resistance that applies in both the smaller prison and the territorial one may force the state to try other measures. So sometimes it acts out those rituals of absolute control by forcing people, citizens, out of the territorial space of the nation state to become anchorless wanderers on the global space. There are the special cases of penal colonies, the most striking being Australia, where a whole people deemed undesirable are removed from one territorial space into another, equally big or bigger. In Africa, there is the example of Angola, which was used as a penal settlement. In a historical note to her translation of Pepetela's novel *Yaka*, Marga Holmes says that in addition to Portuguese colonial officials and troops, 'the white community in the nineteenth century included ex-convicts, political exiles,— Republicans, anarchists,—and some who had fled from the newly Republican Brazil.' Forcing writers and artists into exile is a variant form of penal settlement at the level of the individual. The only difference is that, unlike a penal settlement, the global space where such writers may find themselves is not controlled by the same state. But the spiritual effects might be the same.

IX

A writer floating in space without anchorage in his country is like a condemned person. Nawal el Sa'adawi feels as if she is in jail whenever she is away from her Egypt. For her, exile becomes like another prison. So exile is a way of moving the writer from the territorial confinement where his acts of resistance might ignite other fields into a global 'exclosure'. The hope is that his actions from this exclosure, whatever they are, will not directly affect those confined within the vast territorial enclosure. But here, as inside a prison, there are many contradictions for both the state and the artist. The artist in exile knows that he has been removed from the space which nourishes his imagination. He will nevertheless try to break out of the exclosure and reach into the territorial space. From exile he will still try to challenge the state's absolute hold on the territorial space. And because of this, the state is also in a dilemma. To let an artist go into global space means a continuation of the contest for the attention of a global audience. Besides, the word of the exile may very well travel back to the territory to go on haunting the state. Which is what happened in 1984. Dan Barron-Cohen, an Oxford graduate, and I directed a London production of *The Trial of Dedan Kīmathi* at the Africa Centre using techniques developed at Kamīrīīthū. The Kenya state sought to have the performances, both at the Africa Centre and at the Commonwealth Institute, stopped. They wanted the British government to do it for them, but this time they did not get co-operation. Similarly, in Zimbabwe Ngũgĩ wa Mĩriĩ has utilized and extended the Kamīrīīthū experience to create one of the most continuous community theatre movements in Africa. The Kenyan state tried in vain here too to make the Zimbabwean state act against Ngũgĩ's activities. In other words, the Kenyan state under Moi wanted us all back under its watchful eye in the territory under its control.

That is why banning performances or confining artists in prison or killing them are the actions to which the state frequently resorts. But to avoid the contradictions of prison, exile, and physical elimination, like possible condemnation by the national or international audience, the state may find it much easier to deny the artist space altogether. It is the path that invites least resistance and condemnation, and it is the method highly recommended by Plato: 'And therefore when any of these pantomime gentlemen who are so clever that they can imitate anything makes a proposal to exhibit himself and his poetry, we shall send him away to another city.'[17]

The next city could very well turn out to be a replica of the first, so that the performers could end up being homeless wanderers in search of space.

---

[17] Plato, *Republic*, book 3, in Hofstadter and Kuhns (eds.), *Philosophies of Beauty*, 23.

X

We can now make some tentative observations: that the more open the performance space, the more it seems to terrify those in possession of repressive power. This can be seen through a quick comparison of the actions of the colonial and the post-colonial state to performances in the open space.

The pre-colonial African performance area was often the open space in a courtyard or in an arena surrounded by wood and natural hedge. It could also be inside buildings, as when stories are told in the evening around the fireside. But the open space was more dominant, and even in the intimate circle around the fireside, it is the openness of the performance area that is marked: the story-teller and the interactive listeners are in the same area. Visitors could come into the scene, at any time, for the main door was not barred to would-be guests. Equally well, any of the listeners could go in and out. Any space could be turned into a performance area as long as there were people around. Thus the performance space was defined by the presence or absence of people.

To a certain extent the open space of the pre-colonial African performance has parallels with the social space of the carnival spirit of pre-capitalist Europe of the Middle Ages as described by Mikhail Bakhtin, particularly where he argues that the carnival spirit does not know footlights—that is, it does not acknowledge any distinction between actors and spectators.

Carnival is not a spectacle seen by the people; they live in it and everyone participates, because its very idea embraces all the people. While carnival lasts there is no other life outside it. During carnival time life is subject only to its laws, that is, the laws of its own freedom. It has a universal spirit; it is a special condition of the entire world, of the world's revival and renewal, in which all take part.'[17]

Colonial conquests resulted in clear-cut boundaries that defined the dominated space with controlled points of exit and

---

[17] Mikhail Bakhtin, *Rabelais and his World* (Bloomington: Indiana University Press, 1984), 7.

entrance and the formation of a colonial state to run the occupied territory. And right from the beginning the colonial state was very wary of the open air. It was not sure of what was being done, out there, in the open spaces, in the plains, in the forested valleys and mountains. It was even less sure of people dancing in the streets, in market squares, in churchyards and burial places. And what did those drumbeats in the dark of the night really mean? What did they portend?

The post-colonial state has the same fear of the uncontrolled space, a fear which long ago Euripides dramatized in a confrontation between maenads and the state in the play *The Bacchae*. Pentheus, king of the Theban state, cannot stand it that women are out there in the woods and mountains, beyond the control of the city, even though all they are doing is celebrating Dionysus, the god of wine, whose gifts are joy and the union of the soul with dancing. Darkness in open space is dangerous to women, Pentheus claims, and he vows to use force to bring them back to controllable space within the city. He orders the arrest of Dionysus, and imprisonment in a dark stable, where he will have 'all the darkness that he wants. You can dance in there! As for these women whom you've brought to aid and abet you, I shall either send them into the slave market, or retain them in my household to work at the looms; that will keep their hands from drumming on the tambourines.'[18] The parallels with the authoritarian colonial and post-colonial state are very striking, and that is one of the reasons which may have prompted Wole Soyinka to write an adaptation of it, with a post-colonial African setting, under the title *The Bacchae of Euripides*. Both the colonial and the post-colonial state acted as if they were taking a leaf out of Pentheus's book. The open space had to be limited.

Thus under colonialism there followed attempted suppression or strong limitation of all open-air performances within the territorial space. A few examples from Kenya. I have already mentioned the stoppage of the Ituĩka ceremony. This was one of many such stoppages. After the 1922 Harry Thuku massacre,

---

[18] Euripides, *The Bacchae and Other Plays* (Harmondsworth: Penguin, 1961), 197.

women devised a song and dance sequence called Kanyegenyūri. It needed no permanently defined ground on which it could be performed. The song-poem-dance was banned by the colonial regime: it could not be sung or danced or recited anywhere on Kenyan soil. The colonial state treated another dance sequence Mūthīrīgū, developed after the Second World War, in the same manner. And in 1952 the colonial regime once again acted against the nation-wide upsurge of anti-colonial dances and songs, banning all open-air performances in any part of the country, whatever the performance at a particular moment. Every performance, even a simple gathering for prayers, had to be authorized. Communication between one space and the next had to be authorized. The entire territory was one vast performance space full of threatening motions of innumerable magic spheres. Similarly, in the era of apartheid in South Africa, an elaborate pass system regulated the entire territory as a space for daily performance.

The post-colonial state exhibits similar sensitivities. Collective expressions of joy or even grief outside the watchful eyes of the state, may, in some instances, constitute a crime. So the post-colonial state tries to enact limitations similar to those of the colonial state. In Kenya, under the Chief's Act, a gathering of more than five people, no matter where and on whatever occasion, needs a police licence. The performance space for prayers, funeral dirges, marriage ceremonies, naming tea-parties, family gatherings, sports, are dependent on the issuance of a permit. Thus when the police break into any gathering and break up story-telling sessions in people's homes, they are absolutely within the law. Performances have to be contained in controllable enclosures, in licensed theatre buildings, in schools, especially, but not in open spaces where the people reside.

In other words, says Guillermo Gomez-Peña in his article 'The Artist as Criminal', describing similar scenes of suppression of street performances in Mexico in 1994, 'it is one thing to carry out iconoclastic actions in a theater or museum before a public that is predisposed to tolerating radical behavior, and quite another to bring the work into the street and introduce it into the mined terrain of unpredictable social and political forces'. For as opposed to the official feast of the dominant social forces represented by the state in containable places, the carnivalistic spirit, embodied in the performance of the open space, people's social space, celebrates and marks 'temporary liberation from the prevailing truth and from the established order' and 'suspension of all hierarchical rank, privileges, norms, and prohibitions'. Bakhtin, mindful of twentieth-century state dogmatisms, talked of carnival as 'the feast of time, the feast of becoming, change and renewal' opposed to all that which had been sanctified by the state and declared complete.[19]

A comparison between the first performance of *The Trial of Dedan Kīmathi* on 20 October 1976 within an enclosure of stone and concrete called the Kenya National Theatre and of *I Will Marry When I Want* at Kamīrīīthū village in 2 October 1977 at an open-air theatre, a construction without roof and stone walls, is instructive. The production of *The Trial of Dedan Kīmathi* was by university students in English; that of *I Will Marry When I Want* by a cast of peasants and workers in the Gīkūyū language. Thus in 1976, despite the tensions and the publicity surrounding the productions of *The Trial of Dedan Kīmathi*, and despite the police questions, no action was taken by the state against the performance. But on 16 November 1977 the state banned further performances of *I Will Marry When I Want*. And in 1982 they barred the same Kamīrīīthū group from performing anywhere, even the National Theatre. The government also ensured that the Kamīrīīthū performers would not take advantage of an invitation to perform in the then newly independent state of Zimbabwe by outlawing the group. Moving to the next 'city' was therefore not even an option because to do so they would still have needed passports, and governments do not give passports to groups who do not legally exist.

But the state's reaction to the two spaces is even more instructive. In 1976 and 1982 the post-colonial state could bar people from the National Theatre but the building was never

---

[19] TDR T149 (Spring 1966), 112; Bakhtin, *Rabelais and his World*, 12.

destroyed. In 1982, after the same cast of village actors tried to perform another play, *Mother Sing for Me*, the state reacted, not only by refusing to license the performances but by sending armed policemen to raze the Kamĩrĩĩthũ open theatre to the ground. Again this is so reminiscent of the actions of Pentheus in Euripides' *Bacchae*, written and performed more than 2,000 years ago. Pentheus has just proclaimed his intention to use force against the Bacchantes, for, in his contempt of women, he believes that 'when the sparkle of sweet wine appears in their faces no good can be expected from their ceremonies'.[20] Tiresias, the blind seer, opposes his move against the women's performance in the space of their choice and his reliance on force, warning him that it is not force that rules human affairs. Pentheus is incensed at the seer's resistance, but, unable to inflict bodily harm directly, he orders his men to go to Tiresias' religious performance place, and 'smash it with crowbars, knock down the walls, turn everything upside down, fling out his holy fripperies to the wind. That will sting him more than anything else.'[21] In the same way dictator Moi singled out the women of Kamĩrĩĩthũ for special censure, and then thought to 'sting' all of us where it hurt most by the physical destruction of the Kamĩrĩĩthũ performance space. Performances, not only at the Kamĩrĩĩthũ centre, but throughout Limuru county, were banned. The state attached so much value to the destruction of the open-air space that the whole performance of the ban on the Kamĩrĩĩthũ players on 12 March 1982 was televised for all the country to see. There was the provincial commissioner, with all the regional bureaucrats under him and guarded by armed troops, summoning the village to a meeting where the ceremony denying space to the Kamĩrĩĩthũ players was preceded by prayers from leaders of the various established religious denominations. But it was also noticed that most of the prayers took the form of asking God to endow the human heart with the spirit of tolerance.

[20] *The Bacchae and Other Plays*, 189.
[21] Ibid. 192.

In 1976 Seth Adagala and I could get away with police questioning, but in 1977 I was arrested and taken to a maximum-
security prison for a year, released only after the death of the first
head of state, Jomo Kenyatta; and in 1982 I found myself in exile
from Kenya. The open space among the people is the most
dangerous area because the most vital. Thus the Kenyan state
performance of its ritual of power over the territorial space took
the form of removing me from the people, first by confining me
to prison, and then by forcing me out of the territorial space
altogether. They could have done worse and removed me from
the global space, as happened to Ken Saro Wiwa, and also to
thousands of Kenyans.

                                 XI

The performance space of the artist stands for openness; that of
the state, for confinement. Art breaks down barriers between
peoples; the state erects them. Art arose out of human struggle
to break free of confinement. These confinements could be
natural. But they are also economic, political, social, and spiritual. Art yearns for maximum physical, social, and spiritual space
for human action. The state tries demarcation, limitation, and
control. Two spatial and temporal borders with the inevitable
border clashes between two hostile territories, to paraphrase
Michael Holquist's comment on Bakhtin's characterization of
the state and the carnival in the Middle Ages.[22] Bakhtin's words
are equally applicable to the colonial and post-colonial performance space of both the artist and the state. Carnival laughter,
Bakhtin has written, 'builds its own world versus the official
world, its own church versus the official church, its own state
versus the official state. Laughter celebrates its masses, professes
its faith, celebrates marriage and funerals, writes its epitaphs,
elects kings and bishops',[23] which brings us back to the issue of
rivalry between art and the state in a class society.

[22] Michael Holquist, 'Prologue', in Bakhtin, *Rabelais and his World*, p. xxi.
[23] Bakhtin, ibid. 88.

That is why the question of the politics of the performance space is basic to any theorizing about the post-colonial condition. For the politics of the performance space is much more than a question of the physical site for a theatrical show. It touches on nearly all aspects of power and being in a colonial and post-colonial society. It is germane to issues of what constitutes the national and the mainstream. In a post-colonial state this takes the form of a struggle between those who defend the continuity of colonial traditions and those who want to see reflections of a new nation and a new people in the performance space as a unified field of internal and external relations.

But ultimately the politics of the performance space and its location is a class question. For human labour is the real artist in the world. All other forms of artistic expression imitate that of the human hand and mind. And the human hand and mind have the entire limitless space and time for their performance of the struggle for human freedom and self-realization. But the class society which has come into being has created all sorts of borders, enclosures, to confine that freedom. The enclosures could be the nation state, religions, race, gender, ideology, languages—any social variations on those themes. Questions of the performance space are tied to those of democracy, of civil society, of which class controls the state.

One of the most effective ways of ensuring minority social control of labour and the products of labour is the exclusion of whole classes of people from effective participation in the national life. Whole classes of people can be put into psychic enclosure—slaves and serfs in feudal societies, the working people in most advanced capitalist countries today, and women in most societies. In such societies this is done through what Gramsci described as hegemonic rather than formal exclusionary laws. But in Africa, the exclusion of the majority and their enclosure in narrowed psychic space is achieved through the dominance of European languages. We shall see this when we discuss language, democracy, and a new world order in my third lecture.

THREE

The Allegory of the Cave: Language, Democracy, and a New World Order

I

M Y Kenyan compatriot Ali Mazrui gave his 1966 inau-
gural lecture as Professor of Political Science at
Makerere University on the tantalizing subject of
ancient Greece in African political thought. He could as well
have talked about the same antiquity in African literary practice.
Classical Greece was as integral to English studies as it was to
political science and philosophy. Three of the most frequently
used texts were Plato's *Republic* and Aristotle's *Politics* and *Poetics*.
In another book, *Political Values and the Educated Class in Africa*,
Mazrui has quoted Ugandan sources as claiming that when
Milton Obote, Uganda's first prime minister, was in high school,
his headmaster used to read the *Republic* with the top class every
Tuesday. The writer Okot p'Bitek entitled his book of essays
Artist, the Ruler, an obvious echo of Plato's philosophers as
rulers. And in his autobiography published in 1957, Kwame

Nkrumah tells us that when he returned to Ghana from his studies in the USA, the subject for his first talk to his old school of Achimota, after twenty-two years of absence, was 'The Politics of Plato'. He does not disclose what he told the students, but if we go by what he said of The *Republic* in his *Consciencism*, published in 1964, he must have taken a critical look at what he regarded as Plato's betrayal of the egalitarian ideas of Socrates as manifested for instance in *Meno*, where he takes a slave-boy to illustrate the innate abilities of everyone. The teacher, an Englishman, who had taught him the same text years before and who happened to be in the audience was quick to disclaim any responsibility for the interpretation which Nkrumah now gave to Plato. As for Aristotle, the language of his *Poetics* is to be found in much contemporary literary criticism. In many English departments, the *Poetics* and a number of Greek plays were offered as separate courses or as part of the general study of the development of Western drama. Sophocles' Oedipus trilogy, particularly *King Oedipus* and *Antigone*, have attracted the most attention and intertexual dialogue, most probably because of their themes of fate and defiance. It is not surprising that Oedipus, challenging fate, and Antigone, challenging the state, should have appealed to the African student in an era of intense anti-colonial struggles.

However, it is a little surprising that the *Republic*, given its centrality in Plato's theory of knowledge and in particular the allegory of the cave, given its images of men in chains, has not received as much attention in imaginative literature. As far as I know, only in Ayi Kwei Armah's narrative *The Beautyful Ones Are Not Yet Born*, published in 1968, does this allegory figure prominently in the interpretation of the post-colonial condition in Africa.

The original allegory appears in a crucial section of The *Republic* where Plato is discussing the practicality of his ideal state and the qualities and attributes required of the philosopher-king. The narrator is Socrates. Glaucon and his circle are the participatory listeners to his outline and details of the ideal republic. At one point, Socrates asks them to imagine an underground chamber like a cave, with a long entrance as wide as the cave and open to the daylight. In the cave are men who have been prisoners all their lives. Indeed their feet and necks have been so chained that they cannot turn their heads. They can only look straight ahead of them. Some way off, outside the cave, burns a fire—the source of light—but between the entrance to the cave and the source of light is a screen. Thus for the prisoners in the cave, every object, even their own bodies, appears only as a shadow thrown by the fire on the wall opposite them. It is clear that for such prisoners the shadows become the whole truth until some of them are somehow able to escape from the cave and see the sun, which gives visibility to all objects of sight. Plato highlights their ascent from the realm of the illusionary to that of absolute knowledge, the form of the good, and the necessity of their eventual descent back among the cave-dwellers to help in lighting away the shadows and illusions of their existence. The rest of the allegory is the relationship between the few who have escaped into truth and reality and the rest of the prisoners in the cave.

The allegory is meant to be a vivid visual image of the human condition, its ignorance and the means of its enlightenment. But in the context of colonial domination and resistance, Plato's dark chamber would more likely look like an image of the colonial condition.

In Armah's novel, the reference to the allegory also comes in at a key moment in the narrative. Unable to comprehend truly the enormity of the corruption seething around him in post-colonial Ghana of the early Sixties, the 'hero', simply called the Man, turns to his mentor, a character also simply called the Teacher, for some kind of answer and companionship. The Teacher, who now leads a life of inner contemplation and yoga practices, has actually withdrawn into himself in cynicism and bitterness at the failure of the promises of independence. It is in the context of that failure that he keeps on retelling Plato's allegory.

Why would a Ghanaian novelist in the 1960s turn to ancient Greece for an interpretation of the post-colonial condition, and to Plato in particular? There are very interesting parallels between the Ghana of Armah's time and the Athens of Plato's youth. Plato was disillusioned with the contemporary Athenian politics of his youth and adulthood. In particular he was alarmed at the social instability caused by the alternations of oligarchy and democracy, with neither quite able to deliver on their promises. Years later, in his old age, Plato was to recall in a letter the feelings of his youth, in words and phrases which equally well apply to the feelings of many young people in Africa of the immediate post-colonial moment. He relates how he had been invited to join the oligarchic group which had taken power in 404 BC: 'My feelings were what were to be expected in a young man. I thought they were going to reform society and rule justly, and so I watched their proceedings with deep interest. I found that they made the other regime look like a golden age.'[1]

Not surprisingly the oligarchic committee of thirty is overthrown. There follows a democratic restoration, but during it, in 399 BC, his friend Socrates is executed, a deed which brings about his final disillusionment with contemporary politics and constitutions. In the same letter he describes the period as an age 'which had abandoned its traditional moral code but found it impossibly difficult to create a new one'.[2] The sense of law and morality 'deteriorating at an alarming rate', even under a restored democracy, hastens his disillusionment. He comes to the conclusion that all the existing states were badly governed and that their constitutions were incapable of reform without drastic action, and the only hope of finding justice for the individual and society lay in the reign of true philosophy through either real philosophers gaining political power or politicians, by some miracle, attaining true philosophy. Thereafter Plato devotes his life and times to finding and defining the conditions that could bring about such a just society. The *Republic* is an outcome of that search.

---

[1] Quoted by Desmond Lee, in his introduction to Plato, *Republic* (Harmondsworth: Penguin, 1982), 14.
[2] Ibid. 16

In the same way, Armah's youth, like that of many Africans, was shaped by the promises of change with the overthrow of the colonial regime. Ghana's independence in 1957, the first sub-Saharan African country to get independence, had fired the imagination of the entire continent. Democracy and social justice would reign. Africa would truly be for the Africans. The era of the African personality, touted by Kwame Nkrumah and other nationalist leaders, had come and every single African would be able to walk with his head held high in the streets at home and the world. And then comes the shock of greed and visible consumerism and the instant creation of millionaires on the backs of a million poor. Democracy and socialism become a matter of slogans. How could this, the promise, have grown rotten with such obscene haste, asks the Teacher? 'True I used to see a lot of hope. I saw men tear down the veils behind which the truth had been hidden. But then the same men, when they have power in their hands at last, began to find the veils useful. They made many more. Life has not changed.'[3]

The novel, *The Beautyful Ones Are Not Yet Born*, is an outcome and an expression of that disillusionment. But in its analysis of the rotten, there is an implied search for the basis of a new and more just social system. The beautiful ones, comparable to Plato's incorruptible true philosophers, had not yet been born, but until they were born, society would continue to be ruled badly. And they could be born, because in the Socratic character of the Man—that is, in his pure uncorruptibility—we are shown the possibility of such a birth. Both texts then, though separated by more than 2,000 years, arise from a disillusionment with democracy and the social instability that comes with frequent changes of government, particularly by violent means. In the Athens of Plato's youth, in the late fifth and early fourth centuries BC, democrats were overthrown by oligarchs, who were in turn overthrown by democrats, who were overthrown by oligarchs, and then the oligarchs by democrats again. In Ghana, the

[3] Ayi Kwei Armah, *The Beautyful Ones Are Not Yet Born* (London: Heinemann, 1989), 92.

colonial regime is followed by a democratically elected government and then a military coup, to be followed by so many others
that it is difficult to keep count. And of course the same pattern
is reproduced virtually intact in the rest of the newly independent states.

But though the texts arise out of similar situations of disillusionment, they belong to two historically different times in two
very different societies under very different world situations.
Their use of the allegory of the cave has significant differences.
In both, the dwellers in the cave are more like prisoners. But in
Armah's text Plato's shadows in the cave have become impene-
trable darkness in a deep and cavernous hole. In Plato's text, his
intellectual who escapes from this prison goes through various
stages before he can look straight at the fullness of the sun. In
Armah's text the escaped intellectual sees immediately 'the
blinding beauty of all the lights and the colors of the world
outside. And with the eagerness of the first bringer, the wanderer returns into the cave and into the eternal darkness, and
there he shares what he has, the ideas and the words and the
images of the light and the colors outside'.[4] The dwellers in the
cave reject him as mad; they would rather stay with their eternal
darkness and chains. Plato's intellectual who has come into full
knowledge is reluctant to return to the cave; he has to be
compelled to return to share in his new vision of reality. But
even then he necessarily goes through various stages before he is
able to see through the shadows. For in both the ascent into the
light and the descent into the shadows there is a moment of
blindness. It is as if blindness and insight go together in the
human quest for knowledge. In Armah's text the dwellers
choose darkness even though they now know better. In Plato's
text they are in darkness because they are ignorant, and it will
need the strenuous and continuous presence of the men of
knowledge to eventually persuade the dwellers in the shadows
to turn to the light. It is not a mechanical journey into knowledge. It is in the allegory of the cave where in fact we do see

[4] Ayi Kwei Armah, *The Beautyful Ones Are Not Yet Born*, 92.

Plato's dialectic at work: the play of opposites in the journey of reason to absolute knowledge.

What interests me in both caves is the fact that the intellectual is seen as an interpreter between two realms. Plato admits that the man of knowledge, in his second blindness as he descends from light into the shadows, might become a little confused and might not be able to explain clearly what he has seen, and such a situation might lead the dwellers to kill him, thinking that he was misleading them. In other words, Plato admits the possibility of the intellectual not being able to communicate his ideas in a manner that might make himself be understood. But in Armah's rendering, there is no such possibility. The people seem to understand fully the carrier of the new vision, but they wilfully choose darkness rather than the light of the new vision of freedom and beauty. And hence the Teacher's cynical questions and withdrawal: why should men stand apart and disappoint themselves when people free to choose choose what they want? The question arises, is it not possible that the intellectual is in fact unable to explain the new vision, that he is actually talking to himself, that he confuses talking to himself with talking to the people? What language is the man of vision using in talking to the people in the cave? Is the language spoken by the prisoners in the cave the same as the one spoken by the interpreter? It is possible that Armah is thinking of the middle classes as the only dwellers in the cave, for they are the ones seen as reproducing all the features of the colonial cave so soon after momentary intimations of freedom at independence. But there is nothing in his version of the allegory to lend credence to that interpretation. The whole of post-colonial Ghana, and by implication Africa, is seen as the site of that cave. But even if the middle class was the only social group held prisoner in the cave, it would still be interesting to theorize on the language or languages spoken by the interpreter in the two realms between which he is mediating. In the case of Plato there is no doubt about the language spoken: the difference between the dwellers in his cave and the philosopher-interpreter lie solely in their different experiences and interpretations of reality. In Armah's

cave and in the context of his narrative as a whole it is clear that
English is the language which is being spoken by the interpreter
among the other interpreters and to the people. It is interesting
that a text which is so scornful of the adopted Oxbridge accent
of the Ghanaian middle class should be conspicuously silent on
the question of English as the language used, irrespective of the
accent of the speakers.

II

The role of the African interpreter and of English as a variant of
European languages in the construction of the colonial cave and
of the reproduction of its main features in the post-colonial era
need thorough scrutiny. For in both the colonial and the post-
colonial era the territorial space has become a place of confinement literally and metaphorically, a place where people truly live
in the shadows of poverty, ignorance, and disease even though
they have done everything they could to alleviate their lot. The
peasant and the worker in Africa have done all they could to
send their sons and daughters to schools and universities at
home and abroad in order to scout for the knowledge and skills
which could relieve the community of these burdens but, lo and
behold, each one of them comes back speaking in tongues.
Plato's allegory talks about the shadows in the cave being
produced by light falling on objects and people who pass behind
a screen which stands between the source of the light and the
cave. It is this screen which separates the inside and the outside
of the cave. The screen also functions as a prison gate. In a
colonial and post-colonial situation the screen is made up of
European languages. The interpreter is the only social category
able to see what is on the outside of the screen. This ability puts
him in a position where he can interpret for both sides of the
screen.

I want now to turn to these matters of interpretation and to
look at the genealogy and types of the modern African interpreter. There are three types and three roles into which he could

and has fallen in the colonial and post-colonial era: the interpreter as a foreign agent and messenger, as a double agent, and as a people's scout and guide to the stars of freedom.

III

In 1554 John Lok, an Englishman, made his first voyage to El Mina, a Portuguese trading fort built in 1481, in what is now Ghana. On returning to England he brought back with him five Africans. They were kept in England long enough to learn English. One of them stayed on in London, married an English woman, and settled, and so started the era of African diaspora. By 1601 the number of black people in London was large enough for Queen Elizabeth to issue an edict for their expulsion from the realm. Interestingly, these 'negars and blackamoores' are seen as taking jobs from her white subjects at the time, although it is also possible to see the edict as being motivated by more immediate but sinister needs. The four other Africans, now fluent speakers of the language, returned to Africa as interpreters and public relations men for subsequent English voyagers. Thus according to the account of William Towerson's voyage of 1556, it was one of these interpreters who once pacified a hostile crowd of natives. At first the natives would not come out to meet them in their ship, 'but at the last by the perswasion of our owne negros, one boat came out to us, and with him we sent George our negro a shore, and after he had talked to them, they came aboard our boates withoute feare'.[5] (Note the possessive reference to the interpreter as 'our negro'.) The pattern was established. The region was now ready for the adventures of John Hawkins, who made three voyages in 1562, 1564, and 1567, and in the process ushered in the era of the English participation in the highly lucrative Atlantic slave-trade.

[5] Quoted in Eldred D. Jones, *Othello's Countrymen* (London: Oxford University Press, 1965), 12, from Richard Hakluyt, *Principal Navigations*. This section of the lecture owes a lot to the work of Eldred Jones.

Richard Hakluyt's comprehensive accounts of English voyages all round the world, *Principal Navigations*, came out in three volumes in 1598–1600, and they included the voyages of John Lok, William Towerson, and others. It is said that Hakluyt's publications were acts of patriotism: he wanted to prove that the English were doing as well as the other sea adventures from Spain and Portugal and hence remove the stigma of lack of enterprise on the part of the English. But the accounts also fired the general imagination of Elizabethan and Jacobean writers, Shakespeare and Ben Jonson included, and therefore left a lasting mark on English poetry and prose.[6] Among the many great creations of Shakespeare's imagery, and no doubt inspired by those voyages and discoveries, stands out the celebrated figure of Caliban.

The Tempest, with the focus mainly on Prospero and Caliban, has been worked and reworked in a lot of discourse on the colonial and post-colonial condition. Constant in these is the issue of language. Many such discourses have picked up on Caliban's retort to Prospero's claims of having taught him rational thinking through endowing him with a European language. Caliban basically says that he is using the language to subvert Prospero's hold on the island. But this is only later. By the time Caliban has started to curse, he has already shown Prospero all the secrets of the island, and this aspect of himself is objectified into Ariel. In other words, there has been an Arielite phase in Caliban's relationship with Prospero. Whatever the case, Prospero does not have to learn Caliban's language in order to get to know the secrets of the land. Instead he teaches his own language to Caliban in the tradition of Lok's five Africans. Caliban learns Prospero's language and spies against himself. Like Lok's interpreters he becomes the unwitting accomplice to what happens later: the Atlantic slave-trade and plantation slavery. The same process is dramatized in Defoe's *Robinson Crusoe*, where Crusoe teaches Friday English and the first lesson is that he, Crusoe, is the master.

[6] Eldred D. Jones, *The Elizabethan Image of Africa* (n.p.: University of Virginia Press, 1971), 16.

If the interpreter facilitates his own enslavement through language, the same acquisition functions as a wall demarcating the various plantations. For in the New World, what we now have are plantation islands, territories, spaces, enclosures, rigged up with European names and languages. It is the languages of Europe which define, delimit, and identify each of the plantations in the Caribbean, the Pacific, and the Americas. It is the languages of the different masters which keep them apart, and so prevent the various enclosures from communicating with one another. Spanish enclosures remain Spanish; English, English; and French, French; and these never meet unless through conquest and reconquest. But within each plantation African names and languages are systematically eliminated. Thus, and more crucial for the relationship between diasporan Africans and the continent of their origins, it is the European languages as a whole that worked as a wall, a boundary, far more difficult to cross than that of the Atlantic Ocean. Their linguistic linkage to the mother continent is vitally broken, but that between the plantation-owner and his linguistic base in Europe remains intact.

IV

The same interpreter reappears in the nineteenth century with the direct colonization of the continent. He helps in the conquest of the interior, in mapping out and classifying every corner and resource, and later in the actual administration. The interpreter, the one-way go-between who is actually so by virtue of his knowledge of the master's language, is the soldier, the policeman, the court interpreter, the one that Joseph Conrad described rather contemptuously but correctly as the re-formed African. He is re-formed in European language factories and schools, and he often acts as the carrier of messages. In Conrad's novel *Heart of Darkness*, he is the one who announces, 'Mr Kurtz, he dead', a sentence that T. S. Eliot was to immortalize by using it to introduce the 1925 poems called *The Hollow Men*.

The famous Macaulay minute on Indian education, whose intention was to create a class of Indians who were so in name but English in everything else through linguistic engineering, was clearly a theory which had emerged from practice. Indian bodies with English minds would see the world the same way as their white engineers. The re-formed Indians would become efficient and trusted 'interpreters between us and the millions whom we govern.'[7] The French were to elaborate this into a system they called assimilation, in which some blacks could become French citizens through the same process of linguistic engineering. The French were creating a vast army of Macaulay-type interpreters to help them hold sway over their subjects. The Portuguese and the Belgians followed suit.

It is interesting and quite significant that the main actors in the slave-trade and in plantation slavery were also the main actors in the game of direct colonization of the continent of Africa. So all they did was reproduce the same plantation structures and practices within Africa itself. Colonialism was merely adding historical insult to the historical injury of slave-trade and slavery. Africa became zoned into French, Portuguese, and English regions, which were also linguistic enclaves. And so once again European languages built walls between different regions in Africa, and these walls were often far harder to break than those made of wood and stone and barbed wire. But within each zone the same language wall marked out Macaulay's men in Africa from the rest of the population. A few of Macaulay's interpreters in Africa and in diaspora actually produced books rationalizing the slave and the colonial systems. They became what Edward Said has described in another context as prosecution witnesses for the West. Note that except for the very rare case of Afrikaans in South Africa, the colonizers themselves never lost their linguistic linkages to their home base. The colonial system had learnt well from the

---

[7] Bill Ashcroft, Gareth Griffiths, and Helen Tiffin (eds.), *The Postcolonial Studies Reader* (London: Routledge: 1995), 430.

slave system, whose main features it now reproduced on a world-wide scale.

V

Every phenomenon in nature tends to generate its opposites. The system that was geared to producing one-way interpretation in favour of the slave-owning and colonial presence also gave rise to other contradictory impulses, practices, and outcomes. As happens in history time and time again, the confined do not always accept the conditions of their confinement. They can even turn prison conditions into those of freedom. In the plantations, in the enclosures either in diaspora or on the continent, African languages and their associated images, myths, and stories became the only space in which the slave and the colonial subject were free.

The diasporan African reacted to the decimation of his inherited languages and the imposition of those of the conqueror by creating new languages they variously called patois, creole, or what Kamau Brathwaite now calls nation languages. Their very creations were acts of resistance; and these became sites of further resistance. On the continent, the zone inhabited by colonial subjects and largely marked by African languages became an area of light where it had been assigned to darkness. In their languages they could sing the songs they wanted; they could shout any joy, engage in whispers of love, and organize conspiracies. The state, as we saw in the last lecture, may react vengefully and ban all performances, but often to no avail. In this situation, the allegory of the cave may be read slightly differently. Those in the colonial cave are often whispering conspiracies in their own language about how they can break the chains of ages by breaking down all the walls that prevent the floodlights of the sun reaching their space.

And then out of those interpreting between the gaoled, speaking their own tongues, and the gaolers, speaking their European tongues, arises a new kind of interpreter, the second kind. This one sees his role not as delivering the messages of the gaoler to the gaoled but as articulating the messages and demands of the gaoled to the gaoler. Whereas the first kind is a go-between on behalf of the colonial gaoler, the second one acts on behalf of the gaoled majority. When he talks to the gaolers, it is from the standpoint of the cave-dwellers. In effect, he becomes a spy of the gaoled among the gaolers. He had been to Harvard, Oxbridge, the Sorbonne, Berlin, Lisbon, Rome, so that he knows nearly all the connotations and denotations of their languages. The leader of a revolution, C. L. R. James has stated in his book *The Black Jacobins*, is often one of those who have taken advantage of the language and culture of the oppressor. This is because he knows all the contradictions inside the language and culture of his captors. He was being trained to be a good Macaulay's man, carrying the mind of the English in his black body, but instead he is translating reality from the standpoint of the minds of the dwellers in the cave. He is a double spy. The assimilated begins to curse in exquisite French, to expose the hypocrisy, and to cry out, 'Give me back my black dolls'. By this time he has already become a traitor to his historical calling as a conveyor of messages from the West and a spy for the West among his people. So words like 'traitor', 'ungrateful', 'uppity', are often used against this kind of inter-preter. It is as if John Lok's men had returned to Africa, and instead of doing what they had been trained to do—to help further the cause of English voyages into Africa—they had turned round and warned their people of what to expect and therefore how to deal with the new invasions. Or more accu-rately they had started formulating in perfect English the resistance curses of the people against the newcomers. From this group arose the Jomo Kenyattas, the Azikiwes, the Nkrumahs, and the Awolowos of the colonial world. These often go through the spiritual journey undergone by Caliban: from gratitude for learning to denunciation of the abuses of that learning, which they can do with a perfect command of the language of their master. Their literary prowess was demon-strated in the texts they wrote; for instance, Kenyatta's *Facing*

Mount Kenya, Azikiwe's *Renascent Africa*, and Nkrumah's *Towards Colonial Freedom*.

VI

Allied to this interpreter were those who wrote books and learned disputations. If we disregard St Augustine and Aesop, the earliest of these was Johannes Leo Africanus. He was born in North Africa, as El-Hassan ben Mohammed el-Wazzan ez-Zayyati in about 1494.[8] He became a traveller, a trader, a fighter, an adventurer with much knowledge of Africa and the world, at least within the limitations of time and geography. He was captured by Italian pirates and would have been sold into slavery, but his learning saved him. He was given to Pope Leo X, who in turn gave him his name, language, and religion. And so he was transformed from Hassan ben Mohammed, a barber and Arab-speaking African, into Johannes Leo de Medici Africanus, a Latin-speaking African whose knowledge of Africa exceeded by far any of his contemporaries. His book *A Geographical History of Africa*, published first in Latin in 1550 and translated into English in 1600, gave Europe a far more accurate picture of the interior than the fantastic and ridiculous descriptions hitherto furnished by rumour and oral drama, and aided by more inventions and exaggerations from Herodotus, Pliny, and biblical sources. Leo Africanus' real achievement was to people and humanize a region—filling pre-colonial Africa with real people and real king-doms, where before it had been populated with one-eyed humans without a nose or a face; others with the body of a panther or a lion, or the head of a dog; others with dogs for their kings; and of course the Anthropophagi, the cannibals, of *Othello*. Leo Africanus with his learning, his wide travels, his adventures, his services to the Pope and princes of Italy, is said to have been the original of Shakespeare's Othello. At any rate, Ben Jonson, in

[8] For information on Leo Africanus, I am principally indebted to Eldred Jones. See also Garrett Culhane, 'A Literary Adventure: Explorer Narratives of Africa', MA thesis, African Studies Program, Yale University, Spring 1991.

his introduction to the *Masque of Blackness* performed at the court of Queen Anne at the very beginning of the seventeenth century, in 1605, cited the work of Leo Africanus as among the sources of his knowledge of Africa, and the river Niger in particular.

It is a tribute to Shakespeare's genius that in *The Tempest* he was able to create in the figure of Caliban a character who combined these two interpreters in his body: the one who gives away all the secrets of the island, a spy against himself, and the one who uses the acquired language to articulate his deepest desire for freedom and who talks to Stephano about his island with such love and eloquence. His island is full of noises, 'sounds and sweet airs that give delight and hurt not', an island where 'sometimes a thousand twangling instruments will hum about mine ears'.[9] Here Caliban demonstrates great oral clarity. He could not have done better if he had written and rewritten the words in his own language.

The fictional Caliban and the historical Leo Africanus were to be followed by a whole line of other literary interpreters, particularly in the era of slavery. Leading them was Equiano Gustavuss Vassa, who wrote an account of his life and travels in eighteenth century as part of his contribution to the struggles against slavery and the slave-trade. The book, *Equiano's Travels*, is an autobiographical narrative of his capture as a young boy, his adventures and experiences in slavery and freedom, his struggles for the freedom of his kindred, and his memories of Africa. Like Caliban's retold dreams, his descriptions of the Africa of his remembered childhood scintillate with love and beauty. In the light of what I said in my last lecture about performance as an expression of being, it is interesting that Equiano begins by talking about his community as one of dancers and poets. It is in terms of poetry and performance that he expresses their humanity in direct refutation of Hegel, who in his lectures entitled *The Philosophy of History* uses African performance to prove their subhuman status.

[9] *The Tempest*, III. ii.

African academic and imaginative literature in European languages is a development of the tradition of Leo Africanus and Equiano. It is the literature of the double agent who turns his training as a possible Macaulay's spy to good use as a counter-spy and interpreter of his people to the world. It is the literature of the agent who converts his knowledge of the master's language and culture to articulate, as far as it is possible for him to do so, the submerged world of his people, to translate and interpret the conditions of his people who are crying out for the light of the sun denied to them by the colonial screens built around the cave. The abolition of slavery and, later, independence from colonial rule were the great achievements of the alliance between the second kind of interpreter and his people. As one of Armah's narrative voices articulates so well in *The Beautyful Ones Are Not Yet Born*, 'We knew then, and we know now, that the only real power a black man can have will come from black people.'

VII

But at the moment of triumph something tragically wrong had happened. The interpreter had become captive of the very mastery of the language of the former colonizer. He forgot that his power of accurate articulation came from those black people down there in the cave; and he came to attribute his power to the means of articulation, that is the language of those who had built colonial walls around his people. Holding the reins of power of the post-colonial state, he turned what at best had been a temporary expedient into a permanent necessity. He had become blinded to common-sense reality by the dazzling light and power of his acquired languages. Well, his power had come from talking to Europe and the West, arguing with the metropolis, and why should he not continue with that role? Thus instead of empowering the tongues of those in the cave, the tongues which had really given him the power of prophecy and leadership, he now stood behind the English and French

screens haranguing his people to come out of the darkness of
their languages into the light of European tongues. He also
started talking to them through interpreters because, in
reality, he had never learnt how to speak to the people, how to
hold a genuine dialogue. His real dialogue had been with the
metropolitan bourgeoisie in London or Paris or at the United
Nations.

Here, quite ironically, the interests of the first kind of interpreter and the second coincided. Whether they interpreted from
the standpoint of those in the cave or from the standpoint of the
external forces who wanted to know all about the gold and silver
in the cave, they found themselves, at independence, on the
same side of the linguistic barricade. They could talk to each
other, they could even argue about their profound disagreements, but in English and French. They could disagree on everything, but they were united in believing that real power, real
knowledge, real learning, real being, real unity, real modernity,
came from European languages. What is more, they came from
every ethnic group across the land. In their wilful narcissism
they came to believe that it was they as a social group who
constituted the new nations. So instead of empowering the
languages of those who had given them power, they came to
believe that their power lay solely in their capacity to interpret,
to talk to the West and among themselves about the fate of the
nation. When people said, 'We do not understand you', they
were told to learn English first so that they could understand the
interpreter. Their 'tribal' languages were going to tear the new
nation apart. The two types of interpreters thought that the best
way to achieve progress and modernity was to bring up the new
nations in their own self-image as a class; that is, as a nation of
interpreters talking to the West either in disagreement or in
support—it did not matter, as long as the dialogue and arguments were conducted in the languages of Europe. Their education policies took the form of recruiting sons and daughters of
the various ethnic groups into the middle class of interpreters.
All the available resources of the new nation would go into
strengthening this middle-class core. Gone now was the under-

standing that these languages of Europe had been means to an end. Now they were ends in themselves.

The result of this for Africa is the rise of two nations within the same territory: a small minority speaking and conducting the affairs of the nation in European languages; and the majority speaking their own different African national or communal languages. Alas for the African personality about which Kwame Nkrumah used to talk with so much force; for it was not a unified entity but a split personality.

This has vast implications for the development of the post-colonial nations in Africa. It means literally the split between the mind and the body of Africa, producing what, in my book *Decolonizing the Mind*, I called nations of bodiless heads and headless bodies. The community puts resources into the education of a people who will never bring home their share of knowledge. This has been noted and even dramatized in europhone African writings. In Tsitsi Dangarembga's novel *Nervous Conditions*, Nyamu goes to the mission school to acquire an education which might help to improve his parents' economic situation, but after only one term there he comes back home and claims to have forgotten all the Shona he knew. He can only talk to his family through an interpreter. By the simple means of linguistic engineering he becomes dead to his family. The same phenomenon is observed by Okot p'Bitek in his African-language poem *Song of Lawino* and in the europhone response *Song of Ocol*. Ocol the educated cannot answer even the simplest of questions put to him because his wife does not understand English. She does not exist; she is invisible. Lawino laments her woes and concerns in a song in an African language. She raises questions about performance, economics, culture, religion, education, time, politics; she pleads with him to answer her questions since he is the one who has been educated all the way to a college degree. Yes, Ocol answers her in song—but in English. In this case his answer is a total negation of everything which Lawino symbolizes. He would even ban her language. But this is not the point. His answer, whatever it is, is inaccessible to her. A positive and a negative response, given the language of their delivery, end up in the same wastepaper basket as far as the peasant is concerned.

Now, an intellectual is a worker in ideas using words as the means of production. It means that for Africa the thinking part of the population, the one with the pool of skills and know-how in economics, agriculture, science, engineering, is divorced from the agency of social change: the working majority. At the level of economics, science, and technology Africa will keep on talking about transfer of technology from the West. There are countless resolutions about this in regional, continental, and international conferences. Yet the African intellectual élite, with their *episteme* and *techne*, refuse to transfer even the little they have already acquired into the language of the majority below. The chorus is the same: let them first learn European languages. In the meantime, the game continues: knowledge researched by sons and daughters of Africa, and actually paid for by the entire working majority who need it most, is stored in European-language granaries. There can be no real economic growth and development where a whole people are denied access to the latest developments in science, technology, health, medicine, business, finance, and other skills of survival because all these are stored in foreign languages. Ignorance of progress in ideas is a guarantee against rapid economic growth.

Here we all need a leap of imagination to comprehend the enormity of a situation which we can't otherwise feel because we can all talk among ourselves. I want you to imagine a peasant or a worker in a court of law accused, say, of murder. He is confronted by, say, an English-speaking judge, an English-speaking prosecutor, and an English-speaking defence attorney—and of course an English-speaking interpreter. Lawyering is really an exercise in words and definitions. Even the slightest nuance in a word or sentence can be crucial in determining the outcome of a case. Yet the victim is completely outside the linguistic universe of the justice system about to determine whether he will die or live or spend his life in prison. His plea of innocence or guilt becomes a plea only when put in a language he does not write, speak, or understand. This is true of all the other institutions determining his life. For the entire economic, political, educational, and administrative system, right down to road and market signs, are in English. And we are not talking about one or two years for one or two people. We are talking about the vast majority for the last 100 years. They have been written off the pages of national history and discourse.

Let us go back to the courtroom. The court is in session. Now imagine the privileged position of the interpreter. He is in the same linguistic universe as the judge, the prosecutor, and the defence lawyer. He can also hear the peasant in the dock. Our interpreter may develop the illusion that just because he can hear the language of the peasant he is at one with him, that he is representing him well. The defence lawyer may develop the same illusion. After all, he is truly defending the interest of the peasant. And if he is a good honest lawyer he will fight as well as he knows how. But note that the peasant is not in a position to identify with his own representation either by the interpreter or by the defence lawyer.

The implications for politics in general and democracy in particular are obvious. 'Democracy', démocratie, demokirasia, Ndemokiracĩ, all have roots in the Greek word dēmokratia, a combination of dēmos, people, and kratos, rule. From classical Greece to the present there have been various models of democracy from the direct, like the one outlined in the funeral oration attributed to Pericles in Thucydides' Peloponnesian Wars, to the current varieties of representative democracy, including the socialist model. The constant theme in all of them is the notion of the people, demos, participating in some form or other in the formulation and execution of the rules regulating their lives in society. The most inclusive definition is still the Lincolnian one of the government of the people by the people for the people. There were a number of models for democracy in some pre-colonial African societies, among the Agĩkũyũ of Kenya for instance, which come closest to the notion of rule of the people by the people. Here the model was riikakiracĩ, meaning rule by a generation. In other societies there were mixtures of monarchies and popular control. Again the key concept was the people and their relationship to power. Most Western democratic models have negated the concept of the people because they have all been dependent on slavery: direct, plantation, colonial, wage, domestic, and gender slavery. But they have been able to sustain the self-illusion of democracy by excommunicating sections of the population from the category of the people. And these—not the pre-colonial African ones—are the models often mimicked by the post-colonial state, which literally excludes from the category of the people all those who function in African languages. If you take the more inclusive notion of a people as the working majority, or as all the people in the nation where equality is numerical rather than functional, then it is clear that there can be no democracy where a whole people have been denied the use of their languages, where they have been turned strangers in their own country. The peasant and the worker in Africa have been denied participation in discourses about their own economic, political, and cultural survival. They have no access to information. For democracy to thrive, information must be accessible to all equally. Issues of language inequalities should then be linked to those of social inequalities within African nations themselves. In other words, any search for a new social order within an African nation will have to address the language question.

These issues of language inequalities should also be linked to issues of inequalities between Africa and the West. For in the global context the African people have also been written off the pages of international discourse and history. From the 1884 Berlin Conference which split Africa into various European zones to the present United Nations, Africa exists in international treaties in European languages. At the United Nations and in nearly all its organs, there is not a single African language. The vast majority of Africans become visible in the global power map only through the same national interpreters. Once again there can never be questions of a new world order without the issues of the voiceless majority in Africa being addressed.

A new world order demands at least that the centre from which we look at the world is moved away from its current location in a group of European languages, and recognition in theory and practice that there are other linguistic centres. Take the status of scholarship on Africa. Quite frankly there is nothing so contradictory in African scholarship today, in Africa and in the wider world, than the position of experts on African realities who do not have to demonstrate even the slightest acquaintance with an African language. Have you ever heard, for instance, of a Professor of French at a French university or any other place who did not know a word of French?

The united class of interpreters of the first and second order dominate the post-colonial state. The entire judicial, legislative, and executive arms of the state, and the entire bureaucracy which goes with them, work in European languages. Many post-colonial states have in fact designated European languages as both official and national. This position and policy are a reflection of the narcissim of the African middle class. For in its wilful narcissim, to use Fanon's phrase, this class sees itself as constituting the nation. Thus when some of its spokespeople speak of European languages as now being national and African, it is because they, as a class, see themselves as the content of what is national at the territorial-state level, and what is African at the level of the continent. Since they constitute the nation, then it makes sense that the languages they use are the ones which are truly national and continental.

At the global level, the same class sees itself as part of an European-language-speaking middle class. Thus whether they are merchants, academics, writers, or experts, they have no difficulties in talking to their counterparts at conferences and institutions from Tokyo to New York. And in all these forums they see themselves as representing Africa, that is Africa defined as being constituted of the same class of interpreters.

The fact is that in this position most intellectuals are agreed, and hence they are all at one with the very states of whose actions they may be very critical. The vehemence with which the leading europhone African writers, even those most critical of the post-colonial distortions, have reacted to the possibility of their return to African languages has been remarkable in its unanimity and in its transcendence over the various regions of Africa. If some of the best and most articulate of the interpreters of African total being insist on interpreting in languages not understood by the subject of that interpretation, where lies the hope of African deliverance?

VIII

In Plato's allegory, the philosophers who attained to the clarity of the good, the source of the light and sight of reason which powered the faculty of knowledge, take one or the other of two positions. There are those who do not want to return to the prisoners in the cave below and share their labours and rewards, whether trivial or serious. It would not be surprising if those who had gone so far above the cave were unwilling to involve themselves in human affairs of those in the cave. Plato, or his *alter ego* Socrates, opposes this tendency. This is ironic because in fact the intellectuals who fancy themselves as dwelling in some kind of celestial paradise unconnected with the real world of ordinary struggles would be more in tune with the class assumptions of Plato's imagined republic, where people are more or less permanently divided into castes. In that sense the logic of the allegory of the cave is more in tune with the democratic character against which the entire book is a statement. Democracy would give power to the ordinary person, and Plato, like the rulers of a colonial or post-colonial state, is against this. But his avowed criticism of the imperfect character of democracy—and for him democracy is an example of an imperfect society, along with what he calls timarchy, oligarchy, and tyranny—is contradicted by what he demands of the intellectuals who have attained to the knowledge of the good. What he is calling for is an aristocracy of the intellect, but one committed to holding dialogue with the dwellers in the cave, one which acknowledges the primacy of the people. Hence the second position.

Plato feels that those who have attained the highest possible knowledge in society should be told by the community:

We have bred you both for your own sake and for that of the whole community to act as leaders and king-bees in a hive; you are better and more fully educated than the rest and better qualified to combine the practice of philosophy and politics. You must therefore each descend in turn and live with your fellows in the cave and get used to seeing in the dark; once you get used to it you will see a thousand times better than they do and will distinguish the various shadows, and know what they are shadows of, because you have seen the truth about things admirable and just and good.[10]

In the case of Africa this would involve the entire school and university population. If they returned to the dwellers in the colonial or neo-colonial caves, how would they communicate with the people? They would in fact have to reconnect themselves to the tradition of the third category of interpreters: the interpreter as a scout and a guide. A guide strives to understand and to be understood. This is even more important for the one who possesses knowledge. He strives to be understood.

There is, of course, a way in which every intellectual, every worker in ideas, is an interpreter, no matter what language he is using. In pre-colonial Africa the intellectuals had their base in African-language cultures and histories. There were two types defined by the means of the discourse. There were those in the griot tradition, keepers of the word, keepers of memory of the family and the community, with orality as their means of communication. The ruling councils contained the best minds of their time but were chosen by the community on the basis of character traits observed from childhood and in different stages of their life. Among the Agĩkũyũ such leaders were generally called *athamaki* (plural) and *mũthamaki* (singular). *Mũthamaki* is the nearest equivalent to Plato's philosopher-king, for he led by wisdom, by persuasion, and not by the force of arms. His power of leadership had to do not with wealth or *technē*, but with

[10] Plato, *Republic*. ed. Lee, 324.

language skills. His wisdom showed itself in how he managed words. It was not a matter of sophistry, but one of ruling over matters and problems in such a way that justice was done and was seen to be done. He becomes a kind of interpreter of the collective mind. In such a community Socrates would not have been a stranger, an outsider, but an integral part of its normal functioning. Most likely he would not have been a loner in his questionings and quest for knowledge. We can call this type the oral intellectual.

The culture of the written sign, which goes all the way back to classical Egypt, did also produce its intellectuals, particularly those associated with the medieval universities in Africa. In a speech which he gave at the inauguration of the University of Ghana on 25 November 1961, Kwame Nkrumah cited centres of learning at Walala, Djenna, and Timbuktu as having had singular impact on African education in medieval times. He singled out the University of Sankore as being 'amongst the foremost intellectually inspired of the world'. He then raised the question of what might have been: 'If the University of Sankore had not been destroyed; if Professor Amed Baba, author of more than forty historical works, had not had his works and his University destroyed; if the University of Sankore as it was in 1591 had survived the ravages of foreign invasions, the academic and cultural history of Africa might have been quite different from what it is today.'[II]

Thus by the time of Lok's Africans and the genesis of the first type of interpreter, there was already in existence the third category of the intellectual interpreter, the one who operated within the cultures, histories, and languages of Africa. During the entire slave and colonial periods, this intellectual was superseded by the other two categories, who in fact became even more dominant in the post-colonial period as a national élite linguistically and culturally tied to an international middle class. But although intellectual interpretations in African languages

[II] Kwame Nkrumah, 'Ghana's Cultural History', *Présence Africaine*, 13/41 (1962), 7 and 8.

remained marginalized during the colonial and post-colonial era, the tradition itself remains unbroken.

Whether he was an oral or a literate intellectual, the key thing was that this third category worked in African languages to interpret reality within and without the borders of the country for the consumption of the African community. In the colonial and post-colonial eras it is this type of interpreter who has encountered more problems, particularly where his message was also aimed at the grass-roots of their societies. Unfortunately, and because the education system was geared towards the production of Macaulay's type of intellectuals, not many resources were spent in the production of this third category of the intellectual. African languages, of course, can be used to bring up interpreters on behalf of the enemies of Africa. After all, the first category of interpreter, Macaulay's man, would have had to be a master of African languages as well. But promoting the languages even for the purposes of strengthening that traitorous tradition had its dangers. There was always the implicit fear that any direct dialogue with the dwellers in the cave would not be controllable. Language, any language, was an instrument in the hands of its possessor, and if these languages became the languages of power, would their use always be kept under reasonable control? The fear was that the ideas which articulated and correctly reflected the experience and hopes of the majority could reach the grass-roots. It was Marx who once said that an idea grasped by the masses becomes a material force. And language is obviously the best, the cheapest, and the most effective way of disseminating such ideas. Christian missionaries knew this and translated the Bible into as many African languages as possible. But then it was seen that the people started interpreting the Bible in their own ways, and so where Christianity was meant to be a prison of African souls, it was often used as a key out of the colonial prison. Does the same fear not exist in the colonial and post-colonial era, that if ideas are available in African languages, even anti-African ideas, the people will start developing them in ways that may not always be in accordance with the needs of the national middle classes and their international allies? In Africa and the world, europhone African literature has usurped the name African literature, for instance, and there are hardly any conferences anywhere of those who work in African languages. Foundations within and outside Africa hardly ever fund conferences and seminars conducted in any but European languages, so the work of the third category of interpreters remains marginalized through a combination of state repression and neglect and international indifference. Ali A. Mazrui has made the interesting observation that of the three Nobel Prizes given to Africans since 1986, one was given for work in Arabic and the other two for works in English. Comments Mazrui: 'A Japanese may win the Nobel Prize for works written in Japanese; a South Asian for masterly use of Bengali, Urdu, or Hindi; a Frenchman for genius of expression in the French language; and an Egyptian win for creative accomplishments in Arabic. However, for the foreseeable future, the Nobel Prize for Literature is unlikely to be awarded for brilliant use of an indigenous African language.' According to Mazrui, this is a clear case of 'the linguistic "other"' precluding 'the linguistic "self"' from ever being noticed as being of literary relevance'.[12] Even conferences on African languages and linguistics have to be conducted in English or French to merit financial support. What is being promoted is a kind of collective death-wish for the African-language intellectual tradition.

Nevertheless, it is quite clear that what is required for African development is the re-emergence to dominance of this third category of the intellectual interpreter, and of course a democratic state which would allow, at the very least, equality of space to all the interpreters. Such an intellectual would readily identify with the position of Plato regarding the necessity for those who have acquired knowledge to return to the grass-roots. What is needed is a revolt by all those trained in the traditions of the Macaulay system to reconnect with the dwellers in the colonial

---

[12] Ali A. Mazrui, 'Perspective: The Muse of Modernity and the Quest for Development', in Phillip G. Altbach and Salah M. Hassan (eds.), *The Muse of Modernity* (Trenton: Africa World Press, 1996), p. 5.

and neo-colonial caves and together develop strategies and tactics for breaking free. Such intellectuals, writing and talking in languages which the people can speak and understand, could then bring all the wealth of their contacts with the languages of the world to enrich their own language. For them the maxim in Kwei Armah's novel that their real power would always be that power which came from black people would be an article of faith in theory and practice.

We have glimpses of this intellectual in the actions of Paul Robeson, Kwame Nkrumah, and Julius Nyerere. Paul Robeson was a diasporan African genius: he was gifted in music, sports, and performance. But he immersed himself in the social struggles of the African-American peoples. He was also interested in and followed the struggles of African peoples on the continent. He learnt nine African languages including Yoruba. And Kwame Nkrumah, on coming to power in Ghana, set up a state bureau for African languages. He believed in their development for use in ideas. He believed in their potential. Both Paul Robeson and Kwame Nkrumah died under circumstances that would not allow them to develop further the implications of their choice of actions regarding African languages. It is truly ironic that *The Beautyful Ones Are Not Yet Born* should have been so incisive in its analysis of the post-colonial middle class and so wrong in its assessment of Kwame Nkrumah because the text, in part, was inadequate in its grasp of the machinations of imperialism. It also failed to see that the members of the middle class were trapped not merely within their Oxbridge accents but within the languages of colonial imposition. The class condemned in the text would have found no difficulties in embracing the text and its English linguistic brilliance as an example of their own achievement as a class.

Julius Nyerere is another. He translated Shakespeare's works into Kiswahili and, on coming to power in Tanzania, he made Kiswahili the official and national language. Many of his most important intellectual analyses of the African and world situation were first articulated in Kiswahili. Under his leadership, Kiswahili developed to a point where it can now cope with virtually any aspect of modern science and technology. What is interesting, though, is the emergence of a group within Tanzania who attack Kiswahili and bemoan the loss of dominance of English. This is a group who feel that their membership of the international middle class midwifed by the IMF and the World Bank, and of the international club of civil servants of finance capital, are weakened by the fact that English, though still taught in schools and colleges, is not first among equals in the school and college curricula and in the life of the nation. However, the actions of people like Kwame Nkrumah, Paul Robeson, and Julius Nyerere show the possibility of the re-emergence of this third category of intellectual interpreter to dominance in the life of Africa.

But just now the intellectuals who consitute the third category are still a tiny minority in practice and in influence. They are simply not visible. They are among the *beautyful* ones, anticipated but not yet born. But they have to be born; otherwise Africa, having lost its entire naming system, will become a cultural appendage of Europe.

Such intellectuals, whenever they are born, will grow their roots in African languages and cultures. They will also learn the best they can from all world languages and cultures. They will view themselves as scouts in foreign linguistic territories and guides in their own linguistic space. In other words, they will take whatever is most advanced in those languages and cultures and translate those ideas into their own languages. They will have no complexes about borrowing from others to enrich their own. African intellectuals may have to follow in Armah's footsteps and rewrite Plato's allegory of the cave, but this time applying to themselves the main recommendation to return. They will see their role as that of doing for African languages and cultures what all writers and intellectuals of other cultures and histories have done for theirs.

Unfortunately this is not the main trend in Africa today, where many intellectuals see the use of African languages for discourse as being equivalent to driving a motor vehicle through the rearview mirror, and indeed where African languages themselves still serve as ragged-trousered philanthropists to the languages of Europe. There is a beautiful Greek story about Prometheus stealing fire from the gods to empower humans with the light and heat of science and technology. He is of course punished for so empowering humans. The post-colonial state and intellectual do the opposite of Prometheus: they often steal whatever fire there is to add to the abundance of fires in the West. They steal from the language inheritance of the third category of interpreter to enrich the languages of Europe. We shall see this in my fourth and last lecture, 'Oral Power and Europhone Glory: Orature, Literature, and Stolen Legacies'.

FOUR

Oral Power and Europhone Glory: Orature, Literature, and Stolen Legacies

I

I N my third lecture I said that there was a great need, especially in Africa, for its artists and intellectuals to return to the languages of the people. That statement needs modification. Nearly all African writers have returned to African languages. What they write in whatever language derives its stamina, stature, identity from African languages. Does this claim in any way contradict what I said in my last lecture? Why was I making all that fuss, then, if what I now say is true? This lecture is an attempt to answer that question.

There are three traditions in the imaginative verbal production of Africa. There is that of the linguistic agent: the one who, no matter what the standpoint of his interpretation of its people, history, and culture, used European languages. This tradition has a long history and it goes all the way back to Leo Africanus in the sixteenth century (if we leave out the work of St Augustine and

Aesop) and Equiano in the nineteenth century; although, if we narrow it down strictly to a matter of imaginative reconstruction of reality, it is a twentieth-century phenomenon. In its rise and development, it is closely linked both to the rise of anti-colonial nationalism and to that of higher education in Africa, particularly to the increase in English and French departments. Whether students went abroad for their education or to the colleges in Africa which were anyway linked to overseas universities, they were exposed to the great traditions of European literature. But they were also exposed to the racism within that tradition when it came to the depiction of Africa and its peoples. They revolted against the racism and thought that they could tell their story better. Whether they wrote in French, English, or Portuguese, they went ahead and told it, in poetry, drama, and fictional narratives, so that at independence there was a considerable body of work written by continental Africans in European languages. When allied to that of diaspora Africa—that is, from the Caribbean islands and Afro-America—the consequent black voice was clearly formidable, and it was consolidating itself into a tradition. By the mid-Sixties this tradition had produced a genuine pan-African article: a mirror which, although made from European linguistic glass, was still something that the entire continent and diaspora could claim as their own. In it they could see their faces clearly and hear the genuine voices of their own culture and history. An instance of this is the degree of similarity between Kamau Brathwaite's reaction and my own to the novel *In the Castle of My Skin* by George Lamming published in 1952. Brathwaite is from Barbados, the location of the narrative, and I from Kenya, but we could both see ourselves in this remarkable narrative.

The other tradition, a much older one, is that of Africans writing in their own languages. In East Africa, for example, there has been continuous literary output in Kiswahili since the seventeenth century and even possibly from earlier times. And Amharic in Ethiopia, as a written language, goes back to biblical times. But in terms of imaginative literature, especially fictional and dramatic narratives, the tradition also became stronger with the struggles against colonialism. The reduction of many African languages to the Roman alphabet through the mediation of Christian missions who wanted the Bible to be accessible to the new converts also helped in the growth of this tradition. It is one of those interesting cases and parallels in history that the Bible has played a role in the development of African languages similar to the one it had played in those of Europe after the Reformation. Mazisi Kunene from South Africa, writing in Zulu, Abdulatif Abdalla from Kenya, writing in Kiswahili, and Chief Fagunwa, writing in Yoruba, are part of this unbroken line of writing in African languages. Ironically, this literature does not play the same role in pan-African consciousness as the one in European tongues. What is common in both traditions, though, is the visual mediation of the written sign. The two carry and share the name 'literature'.

The third tradition, the oldest and the most vital, was that of all those works of imagination produced through word of mouth. Here there is no mediation by the written sign. The production line runs from orality straight to aurality: the mouth produces, the ear consumes directly. Historically this goes back to time immemorial and it is still an integral part of the contemporary African reality. In terms of anti-colonial struggles, it has played the most important role. Not surprisingly it is the only tradition against which the colonial state often took firm measures, banning many of the songs and performances, and gaoling the artists involved. This verbal artistic production carries the name orature.

II

The term 'orature' was coined in the Sixties by Pio Zirimu, the late Ugandan linguist. Its emergence in East Africa of the time was a result of the wider debate on the politics of culture and the literary canon which erupted in Nairobi and Makerere, and to a certain extent in Dar es Salaam Universities. English language and literature then dominated the study of humanities in the

African academy; this meant the great periods of English from William Shakespeare to George Bernard Shaw. It was basically a study of the history of English literature and language. But by the time East Africa attained independence from Britain in the early Sixties, the first tradition, of African writings in European languages, was already part of the cultural reality. There was a considerable body of work in English and in English translations, for instance. Why was this not reflected in the teaching of literature and the organization of the departments, asked some of us, particularly Grant Kamenjū in Dar es Salaam, Pio Zirimu in Makerere, and Taban Lo Liyong, Awuor-Anyumba, and myself in Nairobi. What I had in common with Kamenjū and Zirimu, however, was that we were graduates of the same departments at Makerere and in particular at Leeds, where we had had the time and the necessary distance to review and question some of our colonial experiences. With others like Peter Nazareth and Elvania Zirimu from Uganda and Ime Ikiddeh from Nigeria we had emerged as a literary group loosely united by our common interest in issues of culture, literature, and politics. We returned to East Africa within a year of each other. The fire lit by our discussions and association in Leeds was still ablaze in our hearts, and we were ready to ask questions. Ours was the first major challenge to the dominance of the English canon and the Leavisite great tradition in the African academy.

The first shots were fired in Nairobi with a dramatic call in 1968 for the abolition of the English Department. The call has now become a matter of debate and reference in a lot of discourse on post-colonial literature and theory, with sometimes a not altogether accurate representation of it. The call was not for the abolition of English literature as such, but for the reorganization of the English departments so that they would properly reflect the realities of the twentieth century and the world. Why, for instance, should a child study the English novel, instead of the novel in English? English drama, and not a course on drama in English? A rearrangement would allow two things. First it would mean that a student who probably was not going to end up as a specialist in English would have the chance to be acquainted with Tolstoy and Dostoevsky, Flaubert, Stendhal, and Thomas Mann, as well as Dickens and George Eliot. Or, in the case of drama, Molière, Goethe, Aeschylus, Brecht, and Strindberg, as well as Shakespeare and Shaw. Literature in translation then would become admissible. In that case English would be used largely as a means of accessing literature in its different national, cultural, and regional manifestations. It would become an instrument of the study of literature. The restructuring would also allow the introduction of works written in English from other regions and cultures, and this included writings of African peoples. More important was the question of the base. It was felt that for us black literature in general and African literature in particular should be at the centre of any spatial and even temporal linkages to other cultures in Asia, Europe, and the Americas. Central to African literature would be what was then initially termed 'oral literature'.

A secondary debate, but no less intense, was about the place of this oral literature in the academy. What was oral literature anyway? What was more primary, the written or the oral? What was the relationship between orality in general and literacy? For some it was all right to talk about the possible admission of works written in European languages—but why, why 'oral literature', or 'folklore', or whatever 'anthropological' names it had been given?

There were some who saw the oral in terms coined and theorized mostly by anthropologists all the way from Taylor, Frazer, Lévy-Bruhl, to McLuhan, Ong, Goody, and Lévi-Strauss. For these, as for their anthropological mentors, the barbarous, the savage, the primitive, and even the simple were rooted in orality. Why then this retreat into darkness? Surely the oral did not belong to reason, to logic, to history? Orality connoted magic, superstition, and the fleeting: why 'darken' the corridors lit bright by the written sign?

But others argued that orality was the original base of all compositions which had the bodily form of words; that some of the most revered texts, the Bible for instance, had their roots in the oral. It was the invention of movable type by Gutenberg in

1440 which, in leading to the printing-press, had enabled the
literary hegemony over the oral because of its capacity to make
more widely available that which had been on a piece of paper.
Gutenberg had brought the daylight of reason into the dark
night of orality—'so let us cast off the works of the darkness
and take up the armour of light',[1] rang Felix Mendelssohn's
hymn of praise in the 1840 celebration of the birth of the
saint—movable type. It is true that the book, or more accurately
the library, had successfully challenged and undermined age and
even the living as the keeper of memory. But the privileging of
the written over the oral also had roots in the relationship of
power in society and history. Within Europe the rise of the
bourgeoisie and class society had brought about the distinction
between the Mob and the Civilized. The Mob was identified
with the Rural, with women sometimes, and with illiteracy.
Even Karl Marx and Friedrich Engels were driven by the same
prejudice to talk of the idiocy of rural life in their celebrated
Communist Manifesto, which was otherwise so critical of the
capitalist bourgeoisie. The dominant social forces had become
identified with the civilized and the written. With colonization
the same binary opposition was exported to Africa, with the
written and the civilized being identified with Europe as a
whole, while the rural, the oral, and the ahistorical were identified with Africa. The product of the oral no longer belonged to
history because quite clearly the colonizer did not want the
colonized to have any claims to any history as the basis of his
resistance and affirmation of humanity.

The advocates of oral literature argued that the written sign
was only a mediation between orality and aurality; that the oral
still remained subversive of the literary colonizer in that changes
in language—for instance, new words, expressions, borrow-
ings—occur mostly at the level of the oral long before their
conservation in written form; and that, indeed, the literary fed

---

[1] Quoted in Leroy Vail and Landeg White, *Power and the Praise Poem* (London:
James Currey, 1991), 1. Students of orature should find the chapter 'The Invention of
the "Oral Man"' most interesting.

on the living memory of the oral. The great periods of even European literature were those when writers were closest to the oral. Look at Greek literature, Shakespeare, Pushkin and nineteenth-century Russian literature; and was it possible to think of Finnish literature and language without *Kalevala*, clearly a product of the oral? Oral power provided the literary grace in so much of world literature.

The notion of the oral as being central and more basic to the whole aesthetic realm of imaginative arts was gaining ground at Nairobi, and when eventually in 1969 there was a reorganization and a restructuring of the department under the name the Literature Department, oral literature was incorporated into the hallowed grounds of the literary academy. But there was still some disquiet with the term, particularly when the same debate was reproduced in Makerere in 1970.

Oral literature had commonalities with the written. Both were rooted in words. Oral literature was to orality what literature was to literacy. All the genres, the narrative, the poem, drama, which were part of literature were already there in fully developed form in the oral. And because of this there was a tendency to regard the oral as a lower and the written as a higher stage on a progressive linear development. But the oral was not a lower stage. It was a system, a different formal narrative, dramatic, and poetic system. A good example is the rise of the cinematic narrative system and that of cyberspace. These are not developments which turn the other systems—oral and written—into relics of the past in the same way that a technical breakthrough or scientific knowledge may make earlier models and knowledge mere historical curiosities. These systems, while bearing similarities of features, had their own unique characteristics derived from their means of production which differentiated them from each other.

There was performance, for instance, so central to the oral arts but not as readily obvious a feature of the literary. Performance was what made the oral imaginative product so very powerful, be it a riddle, a proverb, a story, a poem, myth, or legend. It was in performance and the conditions surrounding it that a well-developed system of oral aesthetics was perpetually generated. The conditions of the performance were themselves inseparable from the very aesthetic they helped to generate. What were these, the conditions for the self-realization of the oral aesthetic?

There was first of all the architectural space. This could be any open space: *ilo, nja, kĩhaaro,* all these terms carried the notion of the open space. In this open space, the circle was dominant. The circle corresponded to how the moon and the sun looked. The circle was complete; it united all. The performance space also tended to be circular, in a hut or in a compound.

Time frame was also important. In some cultures stories could never be told in day time. They might interfere with the rhythm of work and production. But there were some performance, work songs for instance, which went with the place and time of work or grazing fields. Some performances could take weeks. The Ozidi saga collected by J. P. Clark among the Ijaw-speaking peoples of Nigeria for instance, could take, seven days. Performances to do with rites of passage could also go on for weeks.

One can then imagine the different *mises-en-scène*—call it oral *mises-en-scène*—for the different performances at different architectural spaces and different times of day. One can imagine the play of shadows and light on the bodies and the costumes of the actors. The sources of light, whether the fire, the moon, or the sun, could create different ambiences.

But most important was the audience–performer relationship. The audience could participate as critics and performers. In stories, for instance, a choral phrase or song or response was often taken up by the listeners, who, in so doing, became part of the unfolding of the action. And as the performances were nearly always live, production and consumption affected each other in a very dynamic manner. The oral was connected directly to the aural through performance.

All these conditions were changing all the time so that each performance could never be the same. Each performance was a new imaginative creation. These conditions were very different from those necessary for the aesthetic realization of the written text. Even when the written text was performed, as when drama is translated into theatre, it surely escaped from the world of the literary to that of the oral. The written was clearly a stage somewhere between oral production and aural consumption. It was better to think of the written as storage, a very important storage, but a storage all the same, and reading as the key to that store. The oral text, on the other hand, becomes realizable in its fullest dimension as a work of creative imagination only in performance. So just as writing and reading come to define and underscore the concept of literature, orality and performance assume similar centrality in the aesthetic realization of the oral text. Could performance ever be fully contained and realized in the written? Why then the term 'oral literature', which assumes precisely that incorporation?

It was the difficulties of containing the world of the oral text within that of the literary that led the Ugandan linguist and literary theorist Pio Zirimu to coin the term 'orature'. At first he used it interchangeably with oral literature. But later he was to define the term more precisely as 'the use of utterance as an aesthetic means of expression'.[2] He used it to connote a system of aesthetics, an oral narrative system, for instance, which could be differentiated from the system of visual narratives. The visual systems—from the written to the iconic in the cinema—were in fact seen as more derivative of the oral. Unfortunately he did not live long enough to theorize much more about the coinage and the concept.

[2] This definition is quoted in a paper by Okello-Ogwang, 'Popular Cultural Forms: A Materialist Critique of Gender Representation in the Lang'o Orature', Working Paper no. 42 (Kampala: Center for Basic Research, 1994). He credits this definition to a paper by Pio Zirimu and Austin Bukenya, 'Oralcy as a Tool for African Development', read at Festac 77, Lagos, Jan. 1977. But Zirimu had started using the term as early as 1970 in the debate about the reorganization of the English Department. I am indebted to Carl Sicherman for unearthing several papers in which Pio Zirimu used the term.

III

Not everyone agrees with the coinage. In his very important study *African Oral Literature*, Isidore Okpewho cites the different terms by which 'the subject of our study is identified by various scholars such as oral literature, orature, traditional literature, folk literature, and folklore'. He sides with the term 'oral litera-ture', arguing that it is now the most commonly accepted and that it has turned out to be 'a very useful concept for those scholars interested in examining the cultural relationships between those who can read and write and those who cannot'. Ruth Finnegan, while arguing vigorously for the aesthetic auton-omy of oral literature, or the literariness of oral imaginative productions, does not even mention the coinage in her major work *Oral Literature in Africa*. This is partly because her book first came out in the 1970s, before the word had been coined and gone in circulation. But even in subsequent work and editions there is no reference to it as an alternative to the formulation 'oral literature'.

What's in a name, it might be asked. The debate over defini-tion reminds me of a section in my novel *Petals of Blood*, where two characters argue about names. One of the characters, who has been to school and is acquainted with Shakespeare, para-phrases the famous lines about a rose smelling as sweet even by another name; to which the other character, who is not over-awed by the authority of the English bard, replies that the rose would no longer be a rose because it would be that other name. Names are important signifiers of identity. Their replacements by other names point to different significances. Hence the con-tinuing struggle over terminology. And it is true that with many critics and scholars, the term 'oral literature' holds sway.

Despite this, Zirimu's coinage of 'orature' has taken on a life of its own. Kamau Brathwaite uses the term to describe the productions of what he calls the submerged languages of the Caribbean peoples. A recent major work by Ali Jamle Ahmed, *Literature, Class, the Nation State, and the Politics of Emancipation in Somalia* has a whole section on Somali orature and national identity. Joseph Roach, in *Cities of the Dead: Circum-Atlantic Performance*, has found the term and the concept of orature useful in his intriguing analysis of interactions of the African, Amerindian, and European elements in two sites, New Orleans and London, from the eighteenth century to the present. In Namibia there is an official Namibia Orature Panel under the Ministry of Basic Education. They use the term to refer to 'all areas of knowledge that rely on an oral source, thus encompassing oral history, oral testimony and oral literature'.[3] There is also the Bricks Orature Programme of the Bricks Community Project, whose objective is to 'equip the people at the grassroots level with the necessary information, skills and confidence-building perceptions of themselves so as to enable them to assess their needs, fashion their priorities and participate in the formulation and implementation of development policies'.[4] Most important is the fact that they have started publishing documents under the term 'orature'. Mĩcere Mũgo sees her poems, particularly *My Mother's Poem*, as being rooted in orature aesthetics. In the preface to the Nairobi edition, she acknowledges the influence of orature. 'I wish to pay tribute to those aesthetics and ethics of African orature, as a popular art form, that are positive and progressive,' she writes.[5]

IV

Orature in its suggestive connotations of a system of aesthetics and method and even philosophy was further developed in the Eighties by the pan-African, London-based performance group African Dawn. This group had brought together performing artists from all parts of Africa, but principally from Zimbabwe,

[3] Thiongo Ngũgĩ, *Introduction to Orature* (Windhoek: Namibia Orature Project 1995), 22. This is advertised as the first in a planned series of publications by the Namibia Orature Project.

[4] Ibid. 23.

[5] Mĩcere Mũgo, *My Mother's Poem* (Nairobi: East Africa Educational Publisher, 1995).

Ghana, Senegal, Kenya, South Africa, and Grenada. What attracted them to orature was what they saw as its capacity to encapsulate and integrate different art forms. In the introduction to *Storms of the Heart*, published in 1988, the editor, Kwesi Owusu, tried to use the concept to theorize what was happening to the black arts movement in Britain:

A common point of departure for many black artists is the defiance of formal artistic boundaries, specialization and fragmentation of social experience. There is a conscious articulation of diverse and disparate elements of creativity, often organized in new and exciting spaces. Many black artists work in various media simultaneously, forging creative links, collaborations and alliances. This state of consciousness, a reflection of African and Asian attitudes to creativity, is what is called orature.[6]

Here Owusu, one of the leaders of the group African Dawn, is trying to expand on a statement by the South African sculptor and poet Pitika Ntuli about what orature meant to him and its impact on his work as a poet, sculptor, and performer in exile in Britain. His article in the same book, *Storms of the Heart*, is simply titled 'Orature: A Self Portrait'. Pitika had come from Swaziland, his country of adoption, where, like in his own home, South Africa, 'the fusion of art forms, to be a poet, painter, sculptor, musician, all in one, can be a matter of course. Ceremonies, rituals, fuse all art forms to allow for cross fertilization within the same setting and time.'[7]

Arriving in Britain, he found himself in an environment where everything seemed so disconnected, as if hermetically sealed in different compartments. The new experience made him feel plagued by what he describes as a state of permanent impermanence. He says that he was beginning to feel like a 'deserted man in an arid desert or wasteland of ice' when in 1981 an oasis materialized before him in the form of African Dawn, which introduced him to the concept of orature, the framework of aesthetics within which they were working. His experience of

[6] Kwesi Owusu, *Storms of the Heart* (London: Camden, 1988), 2.
[7] Pitika Ntuli, 'Orature: A Self-Portrait', in Owusu, *Storms of the Heart*, 214.

artistic reality in South Africa and Swaziland now had a name. Pitika explains the impact of the concept on his own practice in London. He talks about how he uses his environment wherever he is to see and make visible the hidden connections between phenomena. He talks of salvaging and humanizing objects, exhaust-pipes, gearboxes, saucepans, curses, insults, appreciation, grey clouds, monotonous terraces, old patches of colour in parks, human touch, frustrations and hopes, all in his war against ugliness. Whatever is around him becomes the raw material for his war. And so, for him,

Orature is more than the fusion of all art forms. It is the conception and reality of a total view of life. It is the capsule of feeling, thinking, imagination, taste and hearing. It is the flow of a creative spirit. Within sculpture alone, it is stone, wood, found objects, metal, shells. In poetry it is not only the images but also their presentation. Orature is the universe of expression and appreciation and a fusion of both within one individual, a group, a community. It is a weapon against the encroaching atomization of life. It is the beginning come full circle on a higher plane. It is a gem, an idea, a reality that beckons us to be part of it.[8]

For Owusu the fusion of art forms characteristic of orature is what gives to black artists an international character as artists and cultural workers defying formal definitions of the geopolitical to connect with centres of inspiration in Africa, Asia, and the Caribbean without relinquishing their claims to their legitimate space within Britain and Europe. Orature so conceived is against the ghetto and the margin. It assumes a dynamic interplay of margins and centres so that one could come to wonder about which was the margin and which the centre. Orature in this sense could even be seen as rejecting the formal boundaries between the written and the oral, between the sign and the icon, or between voices and silences. After all, some silences can be more potent, more menacing, or more promising than anything voiced or made visible by any visual signs and icons. The integrative character of orature is best captured in

[8] Ibid. 215.

Ntuli's description of 'the beginning come full circle on a higher plane'.

V

The interconnection between phenomena captured in the image of the circle, the central symbol of the African aesthetic, is consonant with the materialist metaphysics that one finds in so much of pre-colonial African societies, the remnants of which still condition the African world-view. There is the oneness of nature as the underlying principle of the universe. Whatever is—human beings, animals, plants, birds, stones, air, stars, time, space, and their activities—is an expression of that nature. But nature as the primary order of being generates a second order, nurture, which is social being. For social being is a product of one of the creatures of nature, what in Gĩkũyũ goes under the name kĩũmbe, that which is created, derived from ũmba, create. The human is obviously one of these creatures of nurture. Beyond nature is the supernatural realm, the site of spiritual beings, the highest expression of which is God. And beyond nurture is the super-nurtural realm, the site of spiritual life whose highest expression is the soul. But just as the soul is also in the body and yet beyond the body, God is both within and beyond nature. The four realms of being are another way of conceiving space. Space is a unity containing in itself the four realms: the natural, site of the material force; the supernatural, site of spirituality external to human; the nurtural, site of social force; and the supernurtural, site of human spirituality. Thus the supernatural and the super-nurtural merge in the conception of spirituality and God. No matter how one looks at the four realms, the key thing is their interconnection. They are not completely separate entities. They are connected in the same way that the movement of the entire activity of nature that ends up with rain makes a cycle of being. But each stage in that cycle, cloud formation for instance, or evaporation, has its particular features that distinguish it from the others. Otherwise all the stages are a necessary part of the same circle. The notion of the unity of the circle is also there in the conception of time, particularly in its three broad dimensions of the past *Tene*, the present, *Rĩu*, and the future, *Rũũciũ*. The past is the dwelling-time of the ancestor; the present, the dwelling-time of the living; and the future, the dwelling-time of the unborn. The three are connected, they form another circle of being, and hence in many African libations there is always an invocation of the dead, the living, and the unborn. The child who is born again is a recurring figure in many African cultures. The child is Abiku among the Yoruba of Nigeria, Kariũki and Njoki among the Agĩkũyũ of Kenya. The key in all this is the integrated character of the universe and human existence. Even the notion of time also recalls that of space. One can think of time as diachronic space and space as synchronic time. Thus the dwelling-time is also the dwelling-space, a kind of temporal space. The integrated character of art forms assumed in orature then reflects that of the unity and diversity of the universe. Human beings, in their particularity, are different from animals and plants. But all these forms of being find unity in their dependence on the basic elements of air, water, and fire. Pre-colonial orature in Africa reflects the interdependence of forms of life in the fluidity of movement of characters through all the four realms of being and their interactions in flexible time and space. Plants, animals, and humans interact freely in many of the narratives. Such oral narratives reflect the reverence for life, all forms of life, that is so marked in many pre-colonial African cultures.

VI

Orature then is not seen as a branch of literature but as a total aesthetic system, with performance and integration of art forms as two of its defining qualities. It is more basic and more primary than the other systems of the literary, the theatrical, and the cinematic because all the other systems take one or more of their main features from orature. So while they have their own particularities as means of composition, the four systems cannot

be seen in absolute opposition to one another. It is their hierarchical ordering which is here denied. Otherwise the same
narrative can be told in all the systems observing similar rules
of disclosure to enhance the element of desire to know what
happens next, to fulfil the audience's anxiety of expectation.
Cyberspace, where we can already see the narrowing of the
gap between signs, icons, and voices, is nearer to the world of
the oral. In cyberspace resides the possible merger of the four
aesthetic systems of the written, the oral, the theatrical, and the
cinematic. Cyberspace orature may turn out to be the great oral
aesthetic system of the future.

The centrality of orature to all the other systems calls for a
reconfiguration and regrouping of disciplines. In his book *Performance Theory*, Richard Schechner argues vigorously that it is
more fruitful to see theatre alongside other related activities of
play, games, sports, dance, music, and ritual than alongside
literature, as is the tendency in the usual linkage to literary
drama. The text where it exists is only a key to action and not
its replacement. With theatre alongside them, the seven com-
prise the performance activities of humans. The relations among
them, he argues, obtain not vertically, or originally 'from any
one to the others, but horizontally as autonomous genres'. The
exploration of these horizontal relationships would prove to be
more productive than the search for vertical relationships. In
some ways the most interesting part of the chapter 'Approaches'
is the challenge of the possible reconfiguration of disciplines.
'The possibility exists that a unified set of approaches will be
developed that can handle all performance phenomena, classical
and modern, textual and non-textual, dramatic, theatrical, play-
ful, ritual. Could it be that the historical rifts separating theor-
ists, critics, and practitioners is ending?'[9] The concept of orature
comes closest to meeting that challenge. In terms of the possible
reconfiguration and regrouping of disciplines, drama and the
written text belong to literature, while theatre, music, and
various kinds of performative genres belong to orature.

[9] Richard Schechner, *Performance Theory* (London: Routledge, 1985), 28.

Such a conception of orature transcends the narrow binaries of the written and the oral that condition so much of anthropological and literary thought today. It suggests a transcendence over both the purely oral, the purely literary, and the purely performed. Or perhaps we are prisoners of English language. In the Gĩkũyũ language, the nearest equivalent of the English word literature, *kĩrĩra*, does not carry the notion of the written or of the oral. If I wanted to make the distinction based on the form of composition, written or oral or performed, I would have to add qualifiers to the word *kĩrĩra*. *Kĩrĩra* is everything that enhances human spiritual, moral, and aesthetic strivings. In relationship to the other aesthetic narrative systems, orature, as *kĩrĩra*, stands out as a unifying force.

VII

What is the relationship between the first two traditions which carry the name literature and the third which carries the name orature? The three traditions, the oral, African-language, and European-language writings, coexist today and struggle for their space, in public performances, in the publishing industry, in the academy, in the general scholarship, and in the general imagination. There is also the struggle over which tradition should claim the word 'African' in its purity, without qualification. At the heart of the struggle over definitions and names is surely how Africa should perceive itself, and even how it is perceived in the global community. And how Africa is perceived and perceives itself is at the centre of class politics in the national and international arena. The ruling regimes, the hegemonic Western-educated élite, and the general population will probably adopt different positions. Class ideologies and sympathies and identifications also affect the perception. What is so clearly and undeniably evident is the impact of orature on literature, music, and theatre in all human societies, and in particular on literature, theatre, and cinema from Africa, both europhone and African-language based. The competition, particularly between African literature

and europhone African literature, is not only over which tradition should claim the word 'African', but also over the use and
control of the legacy of orature.

VIII

The contemporary African narratives in European languages—
the europhone African novel—which have made such a distinctive mark in the world are best known for their use of proverbs,
stories, and riddles, which give them an African flavour. In *God's
Bits of Wood*, Sembene Ousmane uses the legend of the Goumba
both to frame and to punctuate his narrative of class struggle in
a colonial context. The legend sang by Maimuona, the blind
woman, tells the story of a contest between man and woman in
the human struggle to tame the land. Their humanity and
human potential are defined not by their gender but by their
relationship to work and to the land. The legend is important to
the entire rhythm, structure, and texture of the novel, where
issues of class, gender, and age interact in the unfolding of the
action and in the determination of the outcome. The same is
true of the work of the Angolan lusaphone writer Vieira, whose
stories *Luuanda* and *One Day in the Life of Domingoes Xavier* are
steeped in elements of orature. The magic realism in the anglo-
phone African narrative that runs all the way from Tutuola to
Ben Okri comes straight from that which surrounds African
orature. Tutuola's *Palmwine Drinkard* and Ben Okri's *The Fam-
ished Road* are inspired by the world of Yoruba orature and the
world-view that emerges from it. And what Chinua Achebe in
Things Fall Apart has said about the proverb, that among the Ibo
it is the palmwine with which words are eaten, is true of a large
body of europhone literary narratives from all over the continent.

The same is true of europhone theatre. Mime, dance, masks,
music, story-telling: all these features of contemporary theatre
are directly borrowed or developed from the traditions of orature. This is true whether one is looking at the rich mime,

dance, and song in the work of Wole Soyinka; or in the story-telling structures that underlie the work of Tess Onwueme, Gcina Mhlophe, and Mohammed ben Abdalla. Many of the theatre artists have explicitly acknowledged their indebtedness to orature. Efua Sunderland is a case in point. She has stated how much she has drawn from the story-telling art, called Anansesem, of the Akan-speaking peoples of Ghana. The name, literally meaning the stories of the trickster figure Ananse, refers to the body of the stories and to their actual performance. An integral part of Anansesem was the accompanying musical performance called Mbogua. 'Many of the Mbogua are part and parcel of the stories themselves and are performed in the context led by the story-teller. But it is a convention for Mbogua to be contributed by other people present. They are permitted to halt the narration of a story to make such contributions, and always their choices are prompted by some sort of inspiration in the performance situation. It is this system of traditional theatre that Sunderland developed, or more precisely, this system from which she borrowed, to create the system she calls Ananse-goro.'[10] Sunderland integrates the Mbogua into her Anansegoro. Although Mbogua is a traditional Akan concept, and she acknowledges that its usage in her Anansegoro has been inherited wholesale, she also uses it to develop action and deepen characterization and to acquaint audiences with the shifts in time and place, and it creates the basis for audience participation. The audience–performer relationship is one of the most important elements of orature. It breaks completely with the fourth wall of the proscenium stage.

Mohammed ben Abdalla has said that for him 'the rituals, dances, music and folklore of our people have a major role to play in the development of African theatre'.[11] He even sees the possibility of developing critical theory from the traditions of orature. He calls upon African playwrights to set their own

---

[10] Efua Sunderland, *The Marriage of Anansewa* (London: Longman, 1987), 4.

[11] Mohammed ben Abdalla, *The Trial of Mallam Ilya*, (Accra: Woeli Publishing Services, 1987) author's preface.

standards, richly drawing from their own cultural heritage, 'our history and the totality of the African experience to create the criteria for judging our own work.'[12]

The two positions are generally representative of the position of many of the practitioners of europhone African theatre: to borrow heavily from the universe of the African creativity to authenticate that theatre as African, expressive of African experience.

It is the same with europhone African poetry. The power and the beauty of the work of Kofi Awoonor and Kofi Anyidoho are in part due to their roots in the world of Ewe orature. There is the special case of Okot p'Bitek, who started with *Song of Lawino* in Acholi. The English translation became very successful and impacted on the development of europhone East African poetry. Thereafter he composed the rest of his long poems directly in English, patterned on the English translation of *Song of Lawino*. However, what gives all his songs their distinctive form and quality is still their relationship to Acholi orature.

The African cinema in whatever language also owes a lot to orature. This is particularly evident in the work of Sembene Ousmane. Sembene sees himself as continuing in the tradition of the griot—in fact he describes himself as a visual griot—a griot using the moving camera to tell his story. The work of Sulemaine Cisse is particularly telling in this respect. His visual poetry in films like *Yeleen* belong to the magic realism of Malian orature.

The same is largely true of literature and theatre in African languages. Here my own case is the opposite of Okot p'Bitek. My first four novels—from *The River Between* to *Petals of Blood*— were all composed in English. And in keeping with their europhone tradition I borrowed flavour from African orature— proverbs, riddles, and legends, for instance. Even the break with the linear narrative structure that many critics have noted in my work after *Weep Not Child* is clearly influenced by the digressional patterns that one finds in a lot of oral narratives. So

[12] Mohammed ben Abdalla, *The Trial of Mallam Ilya*, (Accra: Woeli Publishing Services, 1987) author's preface.

the literary grace in my europhone phase was also derived from the oral power of my cultural inheritance. But after *Petals of Blood*, in the case of the novel, and *The Trial of Dedan Kĩmathi*, in the case of drama, I changed to writing in Gĩkũyũ under circumstances that I have described in my book *Decolonizing the Mind*. This change in the linguistic means of my literary production has affected my work and life profoundly again because of my relationship to Gĩkũyũ orature.

IX

This influence is particularly evident in the practice of Gĩkũyũ-language theatre. The theory and practice of Kamĩrĩĩthũ theatre in the mid-Seventies and early Eighties were based on orality in general and orature in particular. The entire organization, including advertisements, was done orally. Word of mouth was our primary means of communication. This of course had dire consequences for us when the theatre was finally closed, because we had very little to show by way of written records. The play *I Will Marry When I Want*, developed with the workers and the peasants and performed in 1977, borrowed very heavily from the performative elements in orature. The song and the proverb were of particular significance, and they are what mostly attracted the audiences. We sometimes used old songs, particularly work songs, in their original form. But sometimes we would get an old, familiar tune and inject it with new content, and this always jolted the audiences to attention—it had a kind of Brechtian defamiliarizing effect. At other times we would compose new music to old lyrics or simply compose new ones entirely whose form was indebted to the structure of the song in orature. The same pattern of songs was followed in *Mother, Sing for Me*, performed to rehearsal audiences in 1982 before the Kenyan government banned performances in 1982 in the same way as it had stopped those of *I Will Marry When I Want* in 1977. The mime and dance sequences in both productions had a big impact on the audience; and quite often when some members of the audience recalled scenes from the play, it was often the mime that invited imitations and repeated reproductions.

In my Gĩkũyũ-language novels I once again drew largely on orature. *Devil on the Cross* is framed by a Gĩcandĩ performer, for instance. Gĩcandĩ was a form of poetry contest in pre-colonial Gĩkũyũ society. The poets competed in instant narration full of clever riddles that challenged the other poets to respond. In the case of the novel, the narrator is challenging his assumed listeners to find the necessary answers to the many riddles that confront him when looking at the absurdities of post-colonial Kenyan society. The heart of the novel is really a performance. You know the story. In a certain cave in the fictional territory of Ilmorog, there is a competition organized by Satan to choose the seven cleverest thieves and robbers, that is those who steal from the people, not in terms of a few dollars for food, but literally in terms of billions of dollars for the sheer pleasure of accumulating. What each of the thieves has to do is perform stories of his career of theft and robbery before the fictional audience. There is constant interaction between the fictional audience and the performing artists of modern theft and robbery. Not surprisingly, *Devil on the Cross* has been converted into theatre many times in different parts of Africa. The actual narrative unfolds through songs and dramatic settings, and with many of the events orally transmitted. Thus many art forms and genres are utilized in the novel. Repetition of certain motifs is another feature of the narrative, and I borrowed this from the oral narrative.

But the clearest and most deliberate drawing on features of oral narratives is in my novel *Matigari*. I once heard a story being told to my children by one of my sisters. The story, so simple, is of a man who has an incurable wound and is in search of a cure. He is told of a medicine man whose name is Ndiiro, but he does not know the way to Ndiiro's place. He encounters different people and asks each one of them the way to Ndiiro's. The story depends on a repetition of the song that describes Ndiiro. I used the same structure in the construction of *Matigari*, the story of a wanderer in search of social justice in a post-colonial society.

Repetition of key questions and anecdotes is once again part of the unfolding of the narrative.

X

In his celebrated essay 'The Function of Criticism at the Present Time', Matthew Arnold argued that the creation of master works of literature was the result of the encounter between the power of the man and the power of the moment. The man was the possessor of the creative faculty, and the moment, the possessor of elements on which fed the creative. These elements, though the material of creative exercise, were not in its control, argues Arnold, in a statement reminiscent of Marx's famous comment that men made history but not under circumstances chosen by themselves. These elements were more within the critical faculty which in all branches of learning strove to see the object 'as in itself it really is'. Criticism therefore established an order of ideas which, on reaching and permeating the general society, generated 'a stir and growth everywhere' and out of this 'stir and growth come the creative epochs of literature'.[13] Matthew Arnold should have added that it was the world of imagination expressing itself in orality that made the order of ideas current and part of the tissue of life from which the literary imagination drew its blood and stamina. If the critical faculty helped establish an order of ideas, orature established an order of images through which the stir and growth could express itself as part of the general imagination of that society. Great periods of literature drew not only on that order of ideas generated by the critical faculty but also on a legacy of order of images made current in a given moment in society. The pantheon of the gods and spirits of the Greek, Indian, and Yoruba cultures are but a few of the more obvious examples, but in every society there comes a moment when writers are able to draw on the great

[13] Matthew Arnold, *Essays in Criticism* (first pub. London: Macmillan, 1910; repr. edn. New York: Chelsea House, 1983), 4–5.

deposit of images in orature and the world of oral imagination
often inherited from the past. The spirituality of any society is
best expressed through its 'speechuality'.

This is exemplified in the two traditions of writing by Africans
in European and African languages. They depend for their
power and identity on orature. They use oral power to enhance
their literary grace. But orature is a product of African languages. Therefore all this literature is actually dependent for its
identity on that which is produced by African languages. This is
natural and to be expected when Africans write in African
languages. All writers in the world have dealt with the legacies
of their linguistic choice and practice, and one of the greatest
heritages and legacies of human languages is that of orature.
This should be true of African writers as well. Orature is the
great legacy of African life and languages. It is our common well.
And here, in that very fact, lies the problem.

It is the tragedy of the dominant African literary output in the
twentieth century that the exercise and product of the critical
faculty in all the branches of knowledge, the order of ideas, are
stored in European languages, and the great order of images in
the legacy of orature goes to enhance europhone literary rather
than African-language glory. Thus European languages continue
to develop by borrowing not only from their own order of ideas
and images but also from that order of ideas and images generated by African languages. Here in the europhone practice of
twentieth-century African writers is a clear case of a stolen
legacy.

XI

If you look at what is dominant in the academy and in the
general market, it is obviously europhone African literature.
And this literature rightfully belongs to the entire culture and
literature of European languages. What then we are doing is
preying on our own languages to enhance the possibilities of
European languages, and we never give anything back to our

languages. We only know how to take to Europe and to the European language speakers in our own countries, never saying to ourselves: 'What can I give back to my language? What can I do within it, to play my part within it, to extend its possibilities so that others who come after me will also be able to get from it something which I have helped to bring about?' We take from our languages, and the material is processed in European language and resold in Africa as African literature. That is why I have argued, in *Decolonizing the Mind*, that although this literature has contributed to anti-colonial nationalism, to the struggle for human rights, to the exposure of so many ills in Africa, although it has given us all this and more, it is, nevertheless, in its practice, a reflection of the neo-colonial situation. Or rather it is, at the cultural level, a reflection of what is happening at the economic and political level: stealing from the peasant and the worker, and developing Europe. Coffee is grown in Africa, it is processed and packaged in Europe, and then it is sold back to Africa. Gold and diamonds and copper and other minerals are mined in Africa, are processed in Europe, and then resold to Africa. Communication between any two African regions, even neighbouring ones, is often easiest through Europe and America. Is this any different from the literature of Africans in European languages? It borrows from African life and orature, the material of imagination is processed through European languages, and the packaged material in between hard covers becomes African literature. So that even when this literature is at its most denunciatory, it is also an unwitting accomplice to the repressive post-colonial state. Its ideological attitude towards the peasant and what they produce at the level of language and orature is not that different from the attitude of the state and the national merchant and bureaucratic bourgeoisie towards the same peasant and worker. We take their power to enhance literary grace for europhone glory. Orature becomes a stolen legacy alongside other legacies, economic, political, and cultural. Ironically even when this great tradition of orature is researched, conferenced upon, and recorded, it is often done in European languages. Once again Africa produces, the West disposes.

XII

So I come back to the question of the responsibility of Africa's artists and intellectuals to return to the languages of the people. This has been my theme in books, and in my talks, over the last ten years. This is because I do not want the issue to be forgotten. In the context of the language debate, I will remain the gadfly that Socrates was talking about during his trial before the Athenian court. I do of course recognize that the issues are complex, that there are honest disagreements about the paths to take, and that whichever solution eventually triumphs will be long and difficult. There are so many rivers to cross, so many mountains to climb, so many miles to walk. But that is not a reason for ducking the issue and burying our heads in the linguistic sand of Europe, hoping that the language question will somehow pass away. We should take a leaf from the practice of Mazisi Kunene, Abdulatif Abdalla, Chief Fagunwa, and a whole line of others who have kept faith with our languages. We should utilize the oral power of our people for the enhancement of literary grace and the glory of our languages and the people who produced them.

There are challenges and responsibilities, but there are also rewards that go with that choice. A return of the stolen legacies of the people of Africa—from the economic to the cultural—can only empower us African peoples, individually and collectively. Orature, literature, African languages mutually enriching one another will produce the necessary foundations for a new culture of democracy and self-confidence. Oral power will then contribute to literary grace for African languages, creativity, and dignity at home and abroad. The result will be genuine enhancement of oral power and literary glory for Africa.

Concluding Note

I N these four lectures I have talked a great deal about the state of art and the art of the state. I would like to close these lectures on the artist's response to the power of the state and to the challenges of interpretation. The artist can of course choose to withdraw into himself, become silent, self-censor himself, or simply join the ranks of the worshippers at the shrines of the state. In all those he or she would be negating him or herself as a writer for, as I said in my first lecture, a mirror that did not reflect would be negating itself as a mirror. Writers have no real choices other than to align themselves with the people and articulate their deepest yearnings and struggles for change, real change. Where the state silences, art should give voice to silence. Where, for instance, there is no democracy for the rest of the population, there cannot be democracy for the writer. Where there are prisons, the artist is also in prison. Where people are marginalized into ghettos and slums, the artist is also marginalized. Hence it is obligatory for writers in Africa, Asia, South America, and the world over to keep on fighting with the rest of the population to strengthen civil society, expressed in the capacity for self-organization, against encroachments by the state. Hence the struggle for the economic, political, and cultural empowerment of peoples is also a necessary task for the artistic endeavour. The real empowerment of the peoples is the only solid basis for the freedom of the artist. I often sign my book *Detained: A Writer's Prison Diary* for people with the message of my hope for a world without prisons and detention camps. It is the hope, in other words, for a world which will have eliminated the necessity of prisons, detention camps, the army, and police barracks, in short, eliminated the conditions which make the state as we have known it necessary in the organization of human life. It is only then that human civilization will cease to resemble that of the pagan idol described by Marx as drinking nectar only from human skulls.

This may go against the grain of so much of post-modernist rhetoric where hybridity, ambiguity, indecision, the blurring of choices have been elevated to a universal condition. The element of doubt has always been integral to art. Art explores connections even between seemingly unrelated entities. And it is important that human beings become wary of any certainties, particularly those preached and promoted by those with state power. It is important to see, for instance, the connections between the wealth of a few and the poverty of the majority within a nation and between nations. But we should be wary equally about any rhetoric that promotes Hamlet-type indecision about what to think of our societies which produce today baggers of millions on the shoulders of millions of beggars. Or be wary about the language-use that may blunt human social sensitivity to suffering because begging, for instance, is an exercise in free speech or where democratic freedoms are equated with freedom of finance capital. The ascendance of capitalist fundamentalism and the Darwinian ethical system which this is generating poses a singular danger for the world. It is the mother of all the other fundamentalisms, religious and nationalistic, which are developing in opposition to it or in alliance with it. When confronted with the havoc it is wreaking with its religious catechism of 'privatize or perish', it wears the mask of innocence of Graham Greene's Quiet American, or that of one of the comic characters in the American TV comedy *Family Matters*, who will wreak any amount of havoc and then ask, 'Did

I do this?' Rather, there should be no ambiguity about the necessity to abolish the economic and social conditions which bring about the need for charity and begging within any nation and between nations, and language should sensitize human beings to that necessity.

There will always be conflicts between the artist and the state for as long as the state continues to be a supervisor of stabilities erected on gross inequalities within and between nations. Echoing Joubert and probably Shelley, Matthew Arnold once said that force and right were the governors of this world but that force would remain the legitimate ruler until right was ready.

But right is something moral and implies inward recognition, free assent of the will; we are not ready for this right,—right, so far as we are concerned, is not ready,—until we have attained this sense of seeing and willing it. The way in which for us it may change and transform force, the existing order of things, and become, in its turn, the legitimate ruler of the world, will depend on the way in which, when our time comes, we see it and will it.[1]

Paving the ways of seeing and willing a moral universe of freedom, equality, and social justice within and among the nations of the earth is surely the special mission of art. Art is dreams of freedom and creativity.

It is to be hoped that time will come when the state will have been so subjected to the power of civil society that it will wither away, as predicted by Marx and Engels, and simply become a machinery for the administration of conveniences of human social existence. It will wither away in its character as an instrument of class coercion of the majority. And just as it was the case in some pre-capitalist societies, it is possible that in such a post-capitalist society, where production will be geared not towards social domination of others but towards meeting human needs, culture and creativity will reign. But that is in the future. For me, now, art can only play the role of a John the Baptist in the coming-to-be of such a world. It behoves art to join all the other

[1] Matthew Arnold, 'The Function of Criticism', in *Essays in Criticism* (New York: Chelsea House, 1983), 9.

social forces in society to extend the performance space for human creativity and self-organization and so strengthen civil society. It was again Marx who talked about the point of philosophy not being so much to explain the world, as had been the trend hitherto, but to change it. And Martin Carter of Guyana has talked equally eloquently about all those who sleep not to dream, but dream to change the world. The question is, change it to what and for whom? For me, dreaming to change the conditions that confine human life is the mission of art, and it is often in conflict with that of the state as we have known it up to now, in Africa and the world. In such a situation art has the right to take up penpoints, to write down our dreams for a world in which, at the very least, there are no prisons and gunpoints.

Index

creation and creativity 11–12
  inspiration for 17–19
creole languages 83
critical theory/criticism 31, 121–2, 125
culture:
  Agĩkũyũ 8, 11, 12–13, 38–9, 91, 95–6
  Gĩkũyũ 8, 10, 116
  pre-colonial 4, 8–9, 37, 63, 91–2
cyberspace 109, 117

dance 8, 65
Dangarembga, Tsitsi 89
death penalty 35, 54–6, 57, 62
Defoe, Daniel: *Robinson Crusoe* 80
democracy 10, 91–2, 94, 98, 129
Dergue regime (Ethiopia) 25
dreams and dreaming 17–20, 132

East Africa:
  influence on classical world 4, 5
  literature from 105–6, 122
  see also Kenya
education 24, 47, 96
  and language 78, 88, 89–90, 95, 97,
    104
  university studies 104, 105–7, 109
Egypt 2, 4–5, 61
Eliot, T. S. 81
Elizabeth I, Queen 79
Engels, Friedrich 7, 8, 108, 131
English language and literature 78, 104,
  105–7
Equiano Gustavuss Vassa 86, 104
Ethiopia 25
Euripides:
  The Bacchae 64, 67
Europe, *see* colonialism; European
  languages
European languages 69, 78–101
  African literature in, *see* Europhone
    literature
  and colonialism 78–87, 104–5
  democracy negated by 91–2
  knowledge stored in 90–1, 93–4, 126
  in post-colonial state 78, 87–101
  relationship with African
    languages 88, 89, 90–1, 93–4,
    126–7

  see also English language and
    literature; French language and
    literature
European literature:
  African study of 104, 105–7
  and orature 109
Europhone literature 29, 87, 89, 93–4,
  98, 103–28, 119–20
  and legacy of orature 120–2, 126–7,
    128
execution 35, 54–6, 57, 62
exile:
  artists in 35, 61–2

Fagunwa, Chief 105, 128
Fanon, Frantz 93
Fearnow, Mark 54–5, 56
Festac 77 Drama Group 42–3, 49–50,
  111 n.
Finnegan, Ruth 112
Foucault, Michel 54, 55, 58
France: colonialism 82
French language and literature 29, 104
Freud, Sigmund:
  on dreams 17, 18
Frost, Richard 44–5, 48
Fukuyama, Francis 14

Garvey, Marcus 46
Gathwe, Tirus 42
Ghana 72, 73–4, 75–6, 77, 78, 99
Gĩkũyũ language and society
  (Kenya) 8, 10, 116, 119, 123, 124
Gĩthũngũri African Teachers'
  College 47
God 10–14
Gomez-Peña, Guillermo 65–6
Gramsci, Antonio 69
Greece, ancient 4–5, 12, 71–8
Gutenberg, Johannes 108
Haile Selassie, Emperor of Ethiopia 25
Hakluyt, Richard 80
Havel, V áclav 33
Hawkins, John 79
Hegel, Georg Wilhelm Friedrich 13, 86
Hitler, Adolf 21
Holmes, Marga 61
Holquist, Michael 68